Joshua

INTERPRETATION

A Bible Commentary for Teaching and Preaching

INTERPRETATION

A BIBLE COMMENTARY FOR TEACHING AND PREACHING

James Luther Mays, *Editor*
Patrick D. Miller, *Old Testament Editor*
Paul J. Achtemeier, *New Testament Editor*

JEROME F. D. CREACH

Joshua

INTERPRETATION

A Bible Commentary for Teaching and Preaching

John Knox Press
LOUISVILLE

Scripture quotations from the New Revised Standard Version of the Bible are copyright © 1989 by the Division of Christian Education of the National Council of the Churches of Christ in the U.S.A. and are used by permission.

Library of Congress Cataloging-in-Publication Data

Creach, Jerome F. D. (Jerome Frederick Davis), 1962–
    Joshua / Jerome Creach.
        p. cm. — (Interpretation, a Bible commentary for teaching
    and preaching)
    Includes bibliographical references (p.).
    ISBN 0-8042-3106-0
    1. Bible. O.T. Joshua—Commentaries.   I. Title.   II. Series.
BS1295.53 .C74 2003
222'.207—dc21
                                                    2002038080

© 2003 Jerome F. D. Creach
This book is printed on acid-free paper that meets the American National Standards Institute Z39.48 standard. ♾
03 04 05 06 07 08 09 10 11 12 — 10 9 8 7 6 5 4 3 2 1
Printed in the United States of America
John Knox Press
Louisville, Kentucky

SERIES PREFACE

This series of commentaries offers an interpretation of the books of the Bible. It is designed to meet the need of students, teachers, ministers, and priests for a contemporary expository commentary. These volumes will not replace the historical critical commentary or homiletical aids to preaching. The purpose of this series is rather to provide a third kind of resource, a commentary which presents the integrated result of historical and theological work with the biblical text.

An interpretation in the full sense of the term involves a text, an interpreter, and someone for whom the interpretation is made. Here, the text is what stands written in the Bible in its full identity as literature from the time of "the prophets and apostles," the literature which is read to inform, inspire, and guide the life of faith. The interpreters are scholars who seek to create an interpretation which is both faithful to the text and useful to the church. The series is written for those who teach, preach, and study the Bible in the community of faith.

The comment generally takes the form of expository essays. It is planned and written in the light of the needs and questions which arise in the use of the Bible as Holy Scripture. The insights and results of contemporary scholarly research are used for the sake of the exposition. The commentators write as exegetes and theologians. The task which they undertake is both to deal with what the texts say and to discern their meaning for faith and life. The exposition is the unified work of one interpreter.

The text on which the comment is based is the Revised Standard Version of the Bible and, since its appearance, the New Revised Standard Version. The general availability of these translations makes the printing of a text in the commentary unnecessary. The commentators have also had other current versions in view as they worked and refer to their readings where it is helpful. The text is divided into sections appropriate to the particular book; comment deals with passages as a whole, rather than proceeding word by word, or verse by verse.

Writers have planned their volumes in light of the requirements set by the exposition of the book assigned to them. Biblical books differ in character, content, and arrangement. They also differ in the way they have been and are used in the liturgy, thought, and devotion of the church. The distinctiveness and use of particular books have been taken into account in decisions about the approach, emphasis, and use of space in the commentaries. The goal has been to allow writers to develop the format which provides for the best presentation of their interpretation.

The result, writers and editors hope, is a commentary that both explains and applies, an interpretation that deals with both the meaning and the significance of biblical texts. Each commentary reflects, of course, the writer's own approach and perception of the church and world. It could and should not be otherwise. Every interpretation of any kind is individual in that sense; it is one reading of the text. But all who work at the interpretation of Scripture in the church need the help and stimulation of a colleague's reading and understanding of the text. If these volumes serve and encourage interpretation in that way, their preparation and publication will realize their purpose.

The Editors

To Adair and Davis,
Children of the covenant

AUTHOR'S PREFACE

The writing of any scholarly work is, like the Christian faith, a community affair; it cannot be accomplished alone. Therefore, although my name appears on this volume and I am responsible for its flaws, I would be remiss not to acknowledge the many who have made it a better work because of their influence. I am grateful to the editors of this series, James Luther Mays (General Editor) and Patrick D. Miller (Old Testament Editor), for their gracious invitation to write the commentary and for their invaluable insights about addressing the book of Joshua theologically. Moreover, I am particularly thankful that they allowed me to prolong the project because of my transition from a faculty post at Barton College to one at Pittsburgh Theological Seminary.

Many colleagues at Pittsburgh Seminary offered support and guidance. Three of them in particular improved the work by allowing me to glean from their expertise. I benefited from conversations with Ron Tappy concerning matters of history, archaeology, and extrabiblical sources related to the text of Joshua. John Burgess was a ready source of information on matters related to Christian doctrine. I also learned much from my New Testament colleague, Dale Allison. His encyclopedic knowledge of biblical, apocryphal, and pseudepigraphical texts, and his own work on issues of violence in biblical tradition supplied much food for thought, not to mention many leads on secondary sources. In addition to these faculty colleagues, I must thank faculty secretaries Kathy Anderson and Sheryl Gilliland for their help in preparing the manuscript.

Numerous groups listened willingly to my sometimes random and preliminary thoughts on the book of Joshua, and I am grateful for their insights as well. I taught, or co-taught with my wife, Page, portions of the book in three congregations (First Baptist Church, Wilson, N.C.; First Presbyterian Church, Rocky Mount, N.C.; The Presbyterian Church, Sewickley, Pa.) and in a retreat for ministers in the West Hills Ministerial Association, Pittsburgh. A seminar on Joshua and Judges at Pittsburgh Seminary in the spring of 2002 also provided a helpful context in which to test ideas.

Finally, I must thank those who supported this work most extensively, and who sacrificed most for its writing. My wife, Page, gave unflagging encouragement. She also read portions of the manuscript and gave invaluable advice from the perspective of one who regularly preaches the gospel. Our children, Adair and Davis, were a constant source of joy throughout this project, even when they interrupted it! Since the book of Joshua, like Deuteronomy before it, is supremely concerned with passing on the faith to the next generation, it is only fitting that this volume be dedicated to them.

CONTENTS

INTERPRETATION

Introduction

Joshua's Place in the Bible and the Church's Theology

The book of Joshua is one of the Bible's greatest testimonies to the mighty acts of God on behalf of Israel. It reports how the Lord gave Israel the land of Canaan (Josh. 1—12) and allotted it as an inheritance (Josh. 13—19), to fulfill the promises made to Abraham (Gen. 12:7; 15:12–16). This story, along with the book's concluding call to faithfulness (Josh. 23—24), is pivotal to the theology and literature of the Old Testament, no matter how one configures the material. In the divisions of Hebrew Scripture, Joshua is the first book of the Former Prophets. That canonical identification highlights the fact that Joshua promotes obedience to the Law, Genesis–Deuteronomy, which it follows. Indeed, Joshua's opening emphasis on torah obedience (Josh. 1:7–8) establishes the Pentateuch as the primary authority for Israel's life in Canaan and as the basis for the Latter Prophets' (Isaiah through Malachi) evaluation of Israelite society. Furthermore, Joshua 1:7–8, along with Malachi 4:4, helps frame the entire prophetic corpus with injunctions to obey the teachings of Moses.

Scholars have recognized that before the Old Testament was conceived as a three-part collection, and before Joshua was understood as the head of the Prophets, the book was bound in other literary relationships with the material around it. Nevertheless, the two main hypotheses about how Joshua was originally composed confirm the book's central importance. The leading theory is that Joshua initially was part of the Deuteronomistic History, a literary complex stretching from Deuteronomy through Kings that promotes Deuteronomy's sense of religious purity as the standard by which Israel should be judged. In other words, Joshua was intended to be read with Deuteronomy, and only later was separated from it for canonical purposes. Joshua's importance in the Deuteronomistic History, however, is similar to its importance in the Jewish canon. Namely, it inculcates adherence to the teachings of Moses as the primary requirement for Israel's successful life in the land.

Another theory about Joshua's composition is that it began as part of a Hexateuch, which told the story of Israel's salvation, beginning with God's pledge to give Israel the land of Canaan in Genesis 12 and concluding with the fulfillment of that promise in Joshua. This thesis has been largely abandoned as an explanation of Joshua's *origins* (some of the literary links between Joshua and Genesis–Numbers are now thought to be secondary to Joshua's relationship with Deuteronomy, which is stronger and more extensive). Nevertheless, the theory properly acknowledges that the patriarchal narratives anticipate the story of Joshua and are really incomplete without it.

In light of Joshua's central place in the Old Testament story and in the biblical canon, it is not surprising that the book has been a rich theological resource for the church. Traditionally, the Christian community has seen Joshua as foundational for basic doctrines such as election, predestination, and divine grace. As one eighteenth-century expositor put it:

> We see in it much of God, and his providence . . . his faithfulness to his covenant with the patriarchs; his kindness to his people Israel notwithstanding their provocations. (Henry, *An Exposition of the Old and New Testaments*, 2:4)

The church has also found in Joshua a deep well from which to draw its typological expression of the faith. Early Christians saw as significant that Joshua's Hebrew name, *Yehošuaᶜ* (meaning "The Lord Saves") is written as *Iēsous* (Jesus) in Greek. Joshua's attempt to give the Israelites rest from their enemies (Josh. 1:13, 15; cf. 21:44) came to be seen as a model of Jesus' provision of rest from the power of sin (Heb. 4:1–11). In this schema Canaan, the land promised to Israel's patriarchs and possessed through Joshua, symbolizes the heavenly reward of those who follow Jesus. The Jordan, which Israel crossed en route to conquering the land, became a code name for the passage into the next life.

But despite the obvious importance of Joshua in the Old Testament and the traditional place it has held in the Christian community, the book has fallen out of favor with some believers, particularly in the modern period. The problem with Joshua is that it advocates, and says that God dictates, the destruction of all the Canaanites as part of the conquest of the land. This feature of the book seems an approval of what modern people would call "war crimes." In his famous work *The Age of Reason*, Thomas Paine sums up the issue this way:

> There are matters in that book, said to be done by the *express command* of God, that are as shocking to humanity and to every idea we have of moral justice as anything done by Robespierre, by Carrier, by Joseph le Bon, in France, by the English Government in the East Indies, or by any other assassin in modern times. (p. 104)

2

To those who share this view, Joshua represents the worst impulses of humankind, dressed up as an expression of the divine will. As a result of such opinions, some Christians reject Joshua because they think it primitive and brutal, promoting a violent god who is surely different from the Father of Jesus Christ. But perhaps a majority of those who are uncomfortable with Joshua simply ignore it, thus letting the book languish in a kind of scriptural ghetto from which its voice is seldom heard. The revised lectionary gives evidence that this may be the most popular solution to the problem of the book's contents. It includes only a paucity of selections from Joshua, with no story of battle represented (Josh. 3:7–17; 5:9–12; 24:1–3a, 14–25 [Year B has 24:1–2a, 14–18]). But the avoidance of Joshua fails to recognize how indispensable the book is to the larger biblical account. Indeed, the story contained in the book is referred to or quoted directly in fourteen other biblical texts (1 Kgs. 16:34; Pss. 44; 68:12–14; 78:54, 55; 94:4, 5; Hab. 3:11; Acts 7:45; Heb. 4:8; 11:30, 31; 13:5; Jas. 2:25). One thesis of the following exposition is that the contemporary community of faith is impoverished theologically when it fails to attend to Joshua. The commentary attempts to show that this book, with all its objectionable contents, presents a portrait of God and God's demands on God's people that the modern church particularly needs to hear. If the following discussion of Joshua opens doors to that understanding, it will accomplish its primary goal.

The Nature and Plan of This Commentary

This commentary is written for those who teach and preach in the church and its institutions of higher learning. Therefore, those who read Joshua as Scripture will benefit most from the following exposition. The reader no doubt will sense in the commentary empathy for the text and a presupposition that Joshua has potential to edify and call to account the person of faith and the community of faith. That assumption particularly shapes the discussion of violence and warfare in at least two significant ways. First, the commentary recognizes that the obsessive focus on these issues is a modern phenomenon that has, at times, obscured the clear and valuable theological truths of the book. Scholars before the Enlightenment typically saw Joshua's theological claims standing in the foreground and appropriately emphasized them. Therefore, I have found it helpful to consult scholarship that seeks to recover that point of view. In this regard, the work of expositors before the modern era, such as Origen and Calvin, has helped clear away some modern questions that prevent a clear view of the book's theological claims. Second, the discussion of violence and warfare assumes that the book of Joshua has something meaningful and constructive to say about these matters. Of course, such an interpretive lens has the danger of glossing over problems that should be faced. Nevertheless, I hope that a careful reading of

3

Joshua, along with an understanding of Joshua's historical and social contexts, will bear out the truth of my assumptions.

The expository goals of the commentary also impact the selection of issues to be treated and the amount of discussion devoted to them. Some critical questions, such as authorship, stages of writing and editing, and historicity, receive less attention here than in works spawned by the interests of the academy. Critical problems are dealt with insofar as they illuminate the canonical form of the book or as they help the reader better understand Joshua's theological significance. A few more extensive comments on these matters clarify the intentions of the commentary.

1. In the past century scholars paid significant attention to the historical data in Joshua in order to discover, for example, what the conquest account might reveal about the Israelites in the late Bronze Age (1550–1200 B.C.). This commentary does not attempt to reconstruct Israel's taking of the land as a historical phenomenon but instead focuses on how the story of the event works as a story. Those interested in scholarly conceptions of Israel's possession of Canaan (theories of conquest, infiltration, peasant revolt, and the like) may consult the writings of Bright, Gottwald, and Mazar, as well as the commentaries of Butler, Boling and Wright, and Soggin, listed in the bibliography.

2. The problem of Joshua's editorial history too has been the subject of much discussion. The commentary will limit treatment of the issue to those places where it helps illuminate either the present form of the book or some theological issue in the book (see below, "Authorship and Audience," pp. 9–12). The writings of Campbell and O'Brien, Mayes, Nelson, Noth, von Rad, Van Seters, and Wenham provide appropriate resources to begin exploring this question.

3. The commentary assumes, with most modern translations, that the Masoretic Text (MT) is the best witness to the original words of the book of Joshua. The reader should be aware, however, that the Old Greek (that is, the original wording of what we know as the Septuagint [LXX]) contains a better reading than MT in many places. Nelson has treated the evidence thoroughly in his commentary. For additional work on the subject, one may consult the publications of Auld and Greenspoon.

4. Because of concern for the theological significance of Joshua, the commentary devotes significantly more discussion to some portions of the book than others. Although every section of the book receives some treatment, more space is reserved for those units that have been determined important structurally or theologically to the book and that contribute significantly to the thought and life of the church. For example, Joshua 1—12 and 23—24 receive substantially more discussion than

chapters 13—22. The reason for this is simple: although Joshua 13—22 contains some fascinating historical (and even theological) information, lists of tribal territories and boundaries are simply not as replete with theological weight as the speeches of God and Joshua and stories of acquiring and securing the land.

The Nature of the Material: Is Joshua History?

An important question in the study of any piece of literature is, "What type of writing is it?" Joshua is part of a "Deuteronomistic History," but in what sense is Joshua "history"? History writing in the ancient world did not approach the kind of academic exercise it is today. History is never a simple recording of bare, uninterpreted "facts" about the past. A World War II historian may write about particular battles or fighting units in order to give a certain slant on the data, perhaps to inspire courage in the present generation. Nevertheless, modern history writing has conventions of accuracy and documentation that were not practiced widely and consistently among the ancients. Writers such as Herodotus show a concern for sources and verifiability, but there is virtually no sign of such a concern in Joshua. On the contrary, Joshua must be classified as the kind of history that was written in the ancient world to trace national origins and to support nationalistic goals. For Americans, the closest parallels to the kind of history we find in Joshua might be stories of Pilgrims celebrating the first Thanksgiving at Plymouth or George Washington chopping down the cherry tree. Such accounts do not intend to deceive the audience into thinking that something happened that, in fact, did not. And in some cases, they report real event. But their concern is to create identity and teach values, not to report "what really happened." In the process of achieving those goals, stories that have a historical kernel may collapse a complex array of historical events into a simplified account (as with the American Thanksgiving story). Others may be legendary portraits of heroic figures meant to inspire (the George Washington account). The book of Joshua is similar in its goals and content. If it is history, it is what Richard Nelson calls "preached history" (*The Historical Books*, p. 29). In other words, the history in Joshua is composed for theological purposes, not to satisfy the intellectual curiosity of modern readers.

Two examples suffice to illustrate that Joshua should be read primarily as theological literature, not as history in the modern sense. First, Joshua 2—11 portrays rather simplistically the total capture of the land; Joshua 11:23 concludes, "So Joshua took the whole land. . . . And the land had rest from war." Yet, after a summary catalog of conquered kings in chapter 12, God says to Joshua in Joshua 13:1, "You are old and

5

advanced in years and *very much of the land remains to be possessed"* (cf. Judg. 1:1—3:6). Such seemingly contradictory statements can be reconciled when the book is read as theological literature, but not if we insist that it is history in the modern sense of the term. Second, the archaeological data do not square with Joshua's accounts of some cities conquered by the Israelites. In fact, the evidence seems to indicate that many of the battle reports are legendary. The basis of the problem is the fact that the date of Israel's occupation of Canaan can be relatively fixed at 1220 B.C. by the inscription of the name Israel on an Egyptian victory monument called the Mernepthah Stele, created in that year (Israel is listed among those defeated by Mernepthah; see Pritchard, *Ancient Near Eastern Texts*, p. 378). The cities of Jericho (Josh. 6) and Ai (Josh. 8:1–29) seem to have been small, unwalled settlements at that time and throughout the Late Bronze II period (1400–1200 B.C.). Yet, Joshua claims that the Israelites captured and destroyed these cities in major battles. Other cities, such as Bethel, Hazor, and Lachish, do show evidence of significant destruction to defensive structures during the same period, but there is no proof of an immediate repopulation of the sites and little to suggest an Israelite presence among the residents.

It is important to come to terms with the type of history Joshua contains, because it creates a potential theological stumbling block for some people of faith. The problem turns on the issue of whether or not some historical foundation is necessary for faith to be valid. The question arises in Scripture itself (1 Cor. 15:12–19) and should not be passed over lightly. The issue may never be resolved, however, since Joshua's authors did not have the same obsession with history that we have. Moreover, for the modern reader the greatest problem may not be how much of Joshua is historical and how much is not, but Joshua's claims about history itself. Joshua assumes God regularly entered human history and there showed his lordship. But modernity has radically altered this understanding of reality so that, to the modern mind, humans "make" history. Such an imperious self-understanding can render God irrelevant to the historical process. Therefore, a primary challenge for contemporary readers is to enter Joshua's world and to have *our* history and *our* future shaped by it. If we can approach the book in this way, the text may impact us as surely as it did its first readers.

The Theological Context: Joshua and Deuteronomy

As we have said, and as we shall see further in the commentary, Joshua has extensive literary and thematic connections to much of the Pentateuch. Segments of the book perhaps come from Yahwistic and Priestly circles, for example. Joshua is linked most extensively and theologically, however, to the book of Deuteronomy. Therefore, as a general introduction to the theology of Joshua, it is appropriate to focus on those elements of the book that are grounded in the Deuteronomic tradition.

The Mosaic Torah

Deuteronomy 4:44—30:29 contains speeches by Moses that are designated as torah, or instruction. The book indicates that Moses, after delivering his words orally, wrote down the teaching as a deposit of revelation that would act as his surrogate after his death (Deut. 31:9–13, 24–29; 32:44–47). For Joshua, this torah document is the primary authority for Israel's life in Canaan. Indeed, the book opens with Joshua's commissioning ceremony in which God charges Joshua to observe the "law of Moses" (Josh. 1:7). Moreover, Joshua 1:8 makes clear that the torah Joshua follows is a "book," namely, the written document Moses left behind. We see here in Joshua one of the first signs of an awareness of Scripture, a holy text that serves as the primary authority for a community of faith. The permanence of written form makes interesting the fact that Joshua is praised for his complete compliance with Moses' teachings (Josh. 11:15). As we shall see, there are numerous points at which the torah of Moses must be applied or reinterpreted for a new situation. Joshua illustrates that part of Scripture's authority is its dynamic character.

Warfare and the Ban

Joshua shares with Deuteronomy its conception of war in Canaan as a holy endeavor. These books have a particularly strong emphasis on the divine initiative in taking the land. For example, Deuteronomy 20:4 states, " . . . it is the LORD your God who goes with you, to fight for you against your enemies, to give you victory." Of course, the notion of God fighting for Israel is present in many other places in the Old Testament. Nevertheless, Deuteronomy and Joshua have a pronounced view of the land as God's gift to Israel. This is evident when we compare Numbers 33:51–52 with Joshua 13:6. In the Numbers text, Moses is ordered to speak to the Israelites and assure them that "*you* shall drive out all the inhabitants of the land from before you" (Num. 33:52). But in Joshua 13:6 the Lord says emphatically, "*I will myself* drive them out from before the Israelites." This understanding of the land as God's gift provides an important foundation for the conquest story. Because in Joshua it is God's power that wins battles, warfare becomes a kind of ritual for the Israelites. At Jericho the people march in ceremonial order for the divinely prescribed six days, with priests at the head of the procession, and then on the seventh day the walls tumble at the blast of the priests' trumpets. There is no strategy about how to breach the walls of the city, because Israel captures Jericho and Canaan by God's might, not their own military prowess (Josh. 6:8–21).

Particularly important to the theology of holy war also is the concept of "the ban" (Hebrew *ḥerem*) which was to be imposed on Canaanite towns that Israel would occupy (see Deut. 20:16–18). Susan Niditch notes insightfully that the ban is conceived in two ways, as sacrifice and as justice and that both ideas appear in Joshua (*War in the Hebrew Bible*, chaps. 1–2). The first notion, the ban as sacrifice, is based on the recognition that items under the ban are treated like a whole burnt offering; they are totally destroyed, probably by burning (Lev. 27:28–29; Josh. 7:25; 1 Sam. 15:17–21). It also implies that the items declared *ḥerem*, or "devoted things," are rightfully given to God to acknowledge that the Lord acted on Israel's behalf. This applies particularly to the Jericho story, where there is total destruction of the settlement including all its residents, men, women, and children, and the entirety of its living creatures and material goods (Josh. 6:17a, 18, 21). In this instance, the ban may be understood as a prohibition against the retention of spoil as a way of confessing that victory belonged to God. The refusal of all claims on the items and individuals captured could be a constant reminder of who in fact delivered the victory.

The second way of conceiving the ban, as justice, acknowledges that the ban is implemented because of Canaanite wickedness, which might snare Israel and lead to apostasy (Deut. 7). As Walter Brueggemann notes, "The basis of *ḥerem* is not that Israel should not possess, but that Israel should not be seduced" (*Revelation and Violence*, p. 70). In the pagan environment of Canaan, almost all displays of wealth held religious implications, so any of the goods captured in Canaanite cities could encourage idolatry (Deut. 7:2–5). Moreover, the people captured in battle could tempt Israel to adopt their pagan beliefs. After all, the Deuteronomistic historian says that the downfall of Solomon's kingdom was due to his tolerance and syncretistic attitude towards the deities of his foreign wives (1 Kgs. 11:1–13). For these reasons, the Canaanite towns, their residents, and their properties were to be annihilated. This concern for purity and resolute devotion also explains why Israel was to massacre all the people of Canaan—the Hittites, the Girgashites, the Amorites, the Canaanites, the Perizzites, the Hivites, and the Jebusites (Josh. 7:1)—but could offer terms of peace to distant foes who could not influence Israel (Deut. 20:10–15; cf. Josh. 9:3–15). As for the cities that were not part of the God-given inheritance, the Israelites could create vassal treaties, and in such cases, if battle was necessary to conquer a town, they were free to enjoy the spoil of the enemy afterwards (Deut. 20:14). The ban applied only to Canaanite towns and their citizens:

> [A]nd when the Lord your God gives them over to you and you defeat them, then you must utterly destroy them. Make no covenant with them and show them no mercy. Do not intermarry with them, giving your daughters to their sons or taking their daughters for your sons, for that would turn away your children from following me, to serve other gods. (Deut. 7:2–4a)

This theological position could hardly be clearer. And yet that makes the exceptions to the ban, Rahab (Josh. 6) and the Gibeonites (Josh. 9:3–27), perhaps the most important theological segments of the conquest story. The question of why these are preserved will be extremely important in coming to terms with the strange notion of the ban (see pp. 14–18, "The Problem of Violence: A Preview").

All Israel

Joshua, like Deuteronomy, speaks often of "all Israel" gathered for instruction and conquest (Deut. 1:1; 5:1; 11:6; 27:14; 29:9; Josh. 3:7, 17; 4:14; 7:22–26; 8:21, 24; 23:2). The fact that national unity is a real concern in Joshua is evinced by passages that deal with the threat of disunity. This is seen particularly when the Reubenites, Gadites, and the half-tribe of Manasseh settle east of the Jordan. Joshua, just as Moses did before him, cautiously and diplomatically allows the Transjordan tribal groups to live separately, but only after they first aid their kindred in the conquest east of the river (Deut. 3:12–20; Josh. 1:12–15; 4:12). The rather simplified picture of Israel as a monolithic group is striking against the more realistic picture in the book of Judges. There we see intertribal conflicts (Judg. 20) and the failure of some tribes to support military action (Judg. 5). The idealistic picture in Deuteronomy and Joshua is probably influenced by tension between some Israelite groups in the period of restoration. Joshua 22 hints that the land east of the Jordan was considered unclean (Josh. 22:19) and that the tribes who occupied it were of secondary status, a circumstance that probably prevailed late in Israel's history (see the commentary on Josh. 22). For that reason the status of the eastern tribes is highlighted in the book (1:12–18; 13:8–32). Joshua affirms that they are part of Israel and that all the tribes act in one accord.

Authorship and Audience

The book of Joshua gives few clues as to the exact identity of its author. Although tradition holds the book was composed by Joshua himself, a notion supported in a limited way by Joshua 8:32 and 24:26, some features of the book indicate it was written long after the period of Joshua. The most obvious of these is the recurring comment that some practice in the time of the conquest continues "until this day" (Josh. 5:9; 6:25; 7:26; 9:27; 14:14; 15:63; 16:10). Such statements reflect the perspective of an editor far removed historically from the events that are narrated (see Childs, "A Study of the Formula 'Until This Day'"). There are also indications that multiple authors and editors were involved in the process. The book shows evidence of a protracted development: (1) Joshua's farewell speech in chapter 23 seems like a logical conclusion, but it is followed by an account of Joshua gathering the tribes at Shechem for a covenant renewal ceremony in which he again charges the Israelites to be faithful to the Lord; (2) the book seems twice to draw to an end, each time bringing an aged Joshua to his last acts of office, first with a final distribution of the land (Josh. 13:1), second with his final words to the Israelites (Josh. 23:1); (3) the book twice reports that Caleb receives a territorial allotment (Josh. 14:6–15; 15:13–19); (4) the final reports on land distribution in chapters 13—22 differ markedly from earlier accounts of conquest and capture of the land in chapters 1—12; the vocabulary and style within these two distinct sections of the book indicate the work of different authors. Although our purpose here is not to reconstruct each stage of development or the various audiences these stages of growth have behind them, it is helpful to observe that some material in the book appears to be supplementary, producing "seams" in the work. We will offer a sketch of what is likely the earliest version of Joshua and identify two prominent types of additions made to the early work, showing the theological impact these supplements have on the completed book.

The earliest stages of Joshua's formation are probably to be found in chapters 2—11. This section of the book coheres around common interests in the conquest of Benjaminite territory and native connections to the holy site at Gilgal (Josh. 4:19–24; 5:8–9; 10:43). Therefore, it is possible that some form of Joshua 2—11 grew out of that setting. What is more certain is that this section of the current book was incorporated into an early form of Joshua that was originally part of the Deuteronomistic History. The Deuteronomistic editing is particularly evident in Joshua 1; 12; 21:43—22:6; and 23, where these sections supply introductory or summary information in the style of the book of Deuteronomy. They served to frame an early form of the book, likely written for residents of Judah in the latter period of that nation's monarchy, just before the Babylonian exile (587 B.C.). King Josiah (640–609 B.C.) is the likely sponsor of the writing (along with a penultimate form of Deuteronomy, Judges, Samuel, and Kings) because the details of his reign are connected strongly to these portions of the book of Joshua.

The contents and date of subsequent additions to the earliest version of the book of Joshua are hotly debated. What seems clear, however, is that the book was not completed until after the destruction of Jerusalem in 587 B.C. and perhaps not until the residents of Judah returned from exile in 539 B.C. The finished product should be read in the light of the trauma of exile and the identity crises it produced. Although any formal presentation of the editing process is hypothetical, it seems valuable to consider two likely types of additions to the text.

1. Some conspicuous portions of Joshua have a decidedly "priestly" flavor and are somewhat out of step with a majority of the book. This is most obvious in those passages near the end of Joshua that focus on Phinehas and Eleazar. For example, in Joshua 14—19 Eleazar stands with Joshua to cast lots to determine inheritance. In Joshua 22:13–34 it is Phinehas, not Joshua, whom the Israelites west of the Jordan send to settle their dispute with their kindred east of the river. Furthermore, the book concludes with a note about the death of Eleazar, not Joshua (Josh. 24:33)! These additions stand alongside earlier (and more dominant) portrayals of Joshua as a royal figure and serve to temper Joshua's authority. They effectively bring the character of Joshua in the end more in line with the presentation of shared authority of priest and military leader in Numbers 27:20–23; 34:17. To people in exile, who had experienced the failure of royal power to maintain the land, such a juxtaposition of royal and priestly figures may have addressed their doubts about the use, abuse, and limitations of the king.

2. Another important type of addition to the early form of Joshua is a series of comments made about the acquisition of the land: Joshua 1:7–9a; 13:1b-6; 23:6–13. Each of these three sections seems to interrupt a speech about the possession and/or allocation of the land, and each qualifies foregoing or subsequent unconditional promises of land ownership (Smend, "Das Gesetz und die Völker," pp. 494–509). The first and last of these editorial comments set the occupation of Canaan in the context of torah obedience, while the second example raises the awareness that the land is not completely in Israelite hands, despite God's pledge of full control of the territory (Josh. 1:3; 13:7). Similar modifying comments appear also in Judges 2:17, 20–23. Either directly or by implication, each of these statements makes the complete acquisition of the land dependent on unequivocal devotion to torah. Although these segments never deny Israel's God-given right to occupy Canaan, they do limit the claim upon it by making it secondary to the requirement of obedience to the Mosaic law. Therefore, these additions

11

alter what may have been an early emphasis on conquest. In the final form of the book, the greatest concern is a conquest of the heart, that is, torah's demand that Israel be completely devoted to God.

Literary Structure and Unity

To search for "unity" in a book is to look for some logic, some consistency that allows a continuous and coherent reading of the work. At first glance, the book of Joshua seems to have a high degree of disunity. Its three main divisions contribute to this impression: chapters 1—12 contain narratives and speeches that report Israel's entry into the land and possession of Canaan; Joshua 13—22 deals with the allotment of the land; this section features primarily town and territory lists until the narrative in chapter 22 about the conflict between eastern and western tribes; chapters 23—24 present Joshua's final instructions to Israel through a speech (Josh. 23) and a ceremony of covenant renewal (Josh. 24). Particularly the sharp break in style and content between chapters 12 and 13 leads many to conclude that Joshua 13—22 originally had little to do with chapters 1—12.

The section on the allotment of the land may be a late addition to the book, but there are also well-conceived links between these two sections that show they go together quite nicely. Specifically, Joshua 1:1–9 and 13:1–7 contain stylistic parallels that tie the two sections to each other. Both begin with a narrator's temporal comment: "After the death of Moses" (1:1); "Joshua was old and advanced in years" (13:1a). In both cases this is followed by a divine address to Joshua in which the Lord repeats the previous time reference (1:2; 13:1b). Also, in both texts God's speech to Joshua includes a description of the situation Joshua faces, followed by the Lord's charge concerning specific action: "put this people in possession of the land" (1:6); "divide this land for an inheritance" (13:7). These parallels show that Joshua 1—12 and 13—22 were intended to depict Joshua's two primary roles, conquest and allotment of the land, as tandem tasks (note the dual role specified to Israel in Num. 33:50–56). Although Joshua 1—12 and 13—22 may have been composed by different hands, the editors of the book clearly saw them as united in a single portrait of Israel's leader. Moreover, in the final shaping of the book, chapters 13—22 were probably seen as an expansion and explanation of Joshua 11:23 in which Joshua's dual role is summarized:

> So Joshua took the whole land, according to all that the LORD had spoken to Moses; and Joshua gave it for an inheritance to Israel according to their tribal allotments. And the land had rest from war.

In addition to the editorial connections between chapters 1—12 and 13—22, there are numerous other devices that unite smaller portions of the book. For instance, the first three chapters contain a series of references to "three days" that link the installation of Joshua (1:11), the story of Rahab (2:22), and the account of Israel crossing the Jordan (3:2). Such references will be explored further in the commentary on sections where they appear. There is also a series of comments concerning the Canaanite reaction to Israel's presence in the land that helps unite chapters 2—11 (Josh. 2:9–11; 5:1; 9:1–2; 10:1–5; 11:1–5). These statements have a similar structure. Each reports (a) that the people in the land "heard" of Israel's presence and then each reports (b) the Canaanite response. Most important for the unity of Joshua 2—11, these brief comments show a progression from the Canaanites' initial fear of Israel (Josh. 2:9–11; 5:1) to their plans for war against Joshua's army (9:1–2; 11:1–5) and those allied with him (10:1–5; see Stone, "Ethical and Apologetic Tendencies").

On a larger scale, the book contains two recurring themes that help *frame* the whole work and point to matters that are theologically weighty. First, there is an "all Israel" frame. That is, the book's concern for Israel being united fully under Joshua's leadership appears in key places: at the beginning of the book (Josh. 1:12–18); at the start of tribal allotments (13:8–32); and near the end of the work (Josh. 22). The final mention of these tribes shows the greatest overt concern for unity. Joshua 22 reports a rift between the eastern and western tribes created by the eastern groups' construction of an altar by the Jordan. The problem is resolved in chapter 22, and the file closes peacefully on these tribes, but the strategic placement of references to these eastern groups and the content of the final story about them indicate that the Transjordan tribes and the land they occupy is a significant theological issue.

The second framing design for the book is a series of references to torah obedience that underscores a central theological theme in Joshua. This torah emphasis appears first in the opening speech of God, in which God commissions Joshua to be the successor of Moses. The Lord says,

> "Only be strong and very courageous, being careful to act in accordance with all the law that my servant Moses commanded you; do not turn from it to the right hand or to the left, so that you may be successful wherever you go. This book of the law shall not depart out of your mouth; you shall meditate on it day and night, so that you may be careful to act in accordance with all that is written in it. For then you shall make your way prosperous, and then you shall be successful." (Josh. 1:7–8)

13

The topic of torah obedience will arise again, explicitly in Joshua 8:30–35, when Joshua leads Israel in a ceremony to renew the covenant mediated first by Moses. The informed reader will recognize that much of the intervening material also narrates what amounts to a succession of tests of torah obedience. For a positive example, when the Israelites "devoted to destruction by the edge of the sword all in" Jericho (Josh. 6:21), they showed obedience to Deuteronomy 20:10–18; and for a negative example, when Achan retained some of the booty from Ai, he brought trouble upon Israel by defying the same injunction (Josh. 7). At the conclusion of the conquest account, Joshua is evaluated twice according to his observance of the Mosaic legislation (Josh. 11:15, 23; cf. Josh. 11:12). Thus, the whole of the conquest story (Josh. 1—11) is bracketed or "framed" by texts that stress the need to obey the torah of God as handed down to Moses. An additional torah reference extends the torah-obedience theme to the whole book. Namely, in Joshua 23, the penultimate chapter that reports Joshua's farewell address, once again Moses is remembered and revered as the people hear some specific aspects of the Mosaic covenant (Josh. 23:6–13). Much of the language of Joshua 23 is directly parallel to Joshua 1, thus creating a neat frame of references to torah faithfulness.

Joshua 24 does not fit exactly any of these topics that give structure to the book (though it does touch on torah obedience, but not with the same language as Josh. 23). In a sense, it stands outside the frames of the book. But that does not mean that it is somehow detached from or at odds with the previous material. On the contrary, Joshua 24 is so much a summation of Joshua (and in some ways all of Genesis through Joshua) that it draws together most of Joshua's theological interests. That character of the final chapter prevents it from being neatly paired with another segment of the book. It appropriately casts light back on the whole, its entire theological enterprise and call to faithfulness.

The Problem of Violence: A Preview

Before turning to the exposition of specific sections of Joshua it may be helpful to offer some preliminary observations on the issue of violence in the book. The problem cannot be resolved in this brief discussion, and, indeed, it will not be settled in the commentary. But the following comments may prepare the reader for what he or she will encounter in these texts that seem so objectionable.

As with many problems in interpreting Scripture, it is essential for the interpreter to come to terms with the presuppositions at work in the world of Joshua, so that contemporary views of violence are not read back into this ancient book. This will ensure that Joshua is judged

14

on its own terms and that Joshua has the chance to call modern assumptions into question. In this endeavor, it is important to understand the conception of violence that prevailed in the biblical world and how it differs from the notion in our world. This effort is important because, although modern people sometimes use words like "violent" to describe the Israelite invasion of Canaan, the book of Joshua itself does not. That may be due to the fact that the book understands some violent acts as an acceptable part of life, a judgment that many modern people do not share.

There is evidence, however, that the matter is more complex. The Hebrew language does have a word that means "violence" (*hamas*) but carries a slightly different connotation from the English term. In English, "violence" is typically used rather broadly to mean something like exertion of physical force that injures or abuses. Therefore, violence in English can refer to anything from rape to a battlefield assault. The Old Testament seems to understand violence more narrowly; it refers principally to actions that tear at the fabric of Israelite society by defying the sovereignty of God. Violence is spoken of most often in the context of human arrogance and imperious self-interest (e.g., Ps. 73:6). Hence, Israel's conquest of Canaan is not classified as violence since its purpose is to replace godlessness with obedience to God's law. Indeed, according to Deuteronomy, on which Joshua is based theologically, warfare is not simply for the purpose of securing land for Israel. Rather, it is to establish a society based on the torah of Moses, a society in which God will be properly acknowledged as Lord, and humans will act justly towards one another (Deut. 30:15–20). In light of that understanding, it may be helpful to identify Israel's conquest with modern revolutions that have overturned repressive regimes. If the Israelite "conquest" was in part, as some scholars think, a revolt against oppressive Canaanite kings, it *was* an effort to establish justice in the contemporary sense of that term (see the commentary on Josh. 10—12).

These observations are in no way intended as a justification for warfare. It is important to recognize, however, that the Old Testament differentiates between an attack on a city in the midst of war and an attack on one's neighbor or raping a neighbor's daughter (Amos 3:10; Deut. 22:25–27; Jer. 20:8). The latter two actions are examples of violence that the Old Testament detests and legislates against; the former is categorized separately, perhaps as a given part of Israel's existence. The Old Testament has a particular view of violence, and it adamantly rails against what it sees as an unjust offense. The typical vicissitudes and tragedies of warfare are not included in this designation, unless war is motivated by human arrogance (Gen. 49:5–7).

15

It is equally important to understand the modern context in which Joshua is interpreted, a context that has led many to reject Joshua as theologically scandalous. Specifically, it is ironic that some contemporary Christians, particularly in North America and Western Europe, speak against a book like Joshua for its presentation of warfare when they have supported and participated in wars that made the twentieth century the bloodiest period of human history. Of course, many would respond that these wars were intended to stem violence and relieve oppression and thus were "just wars." This seems to be the position of Thomas Paine, who is noted above as condemning the morality of the book of Joshua. Paine wrote in support of the French and American Revolutions as military actions meant to eradicate tyranny, actions he thought were ordained by God. But when such allowance is made for "just" warfare, the contexts of Joshua and of the modern reader may not be as far apart as is sometimes thought, since Joshua assumes that the conquest of Canaan would bring a system of justice.

But the real problem most people have with Joshua's portrayal of war is not that it approves of warfare in general, but that it advocates the wholesale slaughter of the Canaanites. The greatest problem is with the ban, a practice that seems eerily similar to modern examples of genocide. But here too Joshua has been misread in two ways. First, it has often been understood as a historical account of what an Israelite army actually did. In reality, the battle reports we find in the book are mostly aggrandized by authors living centuries after the events. As we have already seen, archaeological evidence shows Joshua contains narratives that may not be considered historically accurate by modern standards. In other words, Israel did not in reality commit genocide (at least to the extent and of the nature reported in the book), as the text of Joshua itself tells us, upon close reading (see Josh. 13:1–6; Judg. 3:1–6).

Second, the people who composed the book of Joshua were hardly citizens of a political superpower, mightily equipped to dominate their world. In fact, the Old Testament sometimes labels the military actions of such nations "violence" (Joel 4:19). Instead, Joshua's audience had a history littered with experiences of being victimized, made homeless, enslaved, and controlled by the major empires of their day. By the time the book of Joshua was completed, both Israel and Judah had been attacked, politically and militarily exploited, and exiled by the likes of Egypt, Babylon, and Assyria. Furthermore, in the five hundred years after this book's composition, these people would be dwarfed and domineered by the Medo-Persian empire, Alexander the Great and the Greeks, and the Romans. The grand reports of Israel annihilating the

16

Canaanites must be read in part as an attempt to present an Israel that was more powerful than was true historically.

Critics have often pointed out that, as important as the historical perspective just described is, the ban still remains in the text of Joshua. That is a fair observation, for indeed the ban plays an important role in the book. But the manner in which the ban is presented in Joshua has not been treated adequately. Only a few scholars have noticed the signs of discomfort with the ban in the book itself and the attempt of Joshua's authors to soften the traditions about the ban or even to abrogate them altogether. Their attempts to do so may be illustrated by two examples.

First, as we have already observed, a series of comments on the Canaanite reaction to Israel's presence in the land cast the conquest as an almost defensive action (see Stone, "Ethical and Apologetic Tendencies"). These brief passages show a progression from the Canaanites' initial fear of Israel (Josh. 2:9–11; 5:1) to their plans for war against Joshua's army (9:1–2; 11:1–5) and those allied with him (10:1–5). Hence, Joshua 10—12, which contains the most extensive description of Israel's slaughter of the Canaanites, depicts the entire Israelite action, after the defeat of Jericho and Ai, as a response to Canaanite aggression and as a defense of the Gibeonites, with whom Israel is bound in covenant (Josh. 9:3–27).

Second, most significantly, this section of the book concludes by saying, "There was not a town that made peace with the Israelites, except the Hivites, the inhabitants of Gibeon; all were taken in battle" (Josh. 11:19). The statement is curious, since the Deuteronomic law stipulates that all Canaanites in towns Israel will occupy are to be destroyed. Yet it sounds as though there was actually a chance for peace, but the Canaanites refused to accept it. That in fact is how one rabbinical tradition understood the verse, and there is good reason to read the whole conquest story with that assumption (Hoffman, "The Deuteronomic Conception of Herem"). As Ellen Davis has pointed out, the only Canaanites who are not faceless in the story are spared the ban ("Critical Traditioning"). Although Rahab and the Gibeonites gain their salvation through manipulation and trickery, still the emphasis of the story is on their preservation. They both profess the universal sovereignty of Israel's God (Josh. 2:11; 9:9–10), which seems to be the primary requirement for membership in the covenant community (see the commentary on Josh. 22). Indeed, these Canaanites display a stance in life that prevents violence, unlike their neighbors who refuse to acknowledge God's power and their dependence on his mercy.

To be sure, the ban remains for modern Christians a strange and reprehensible element of ancient warfare and of the book of Joshua. It

17

is also difficult to understand why the ban was so essential a part of the Deuteronomic tradition. Despite these difficulties, however, it is important to recognize that Joshua's authors wrestle with the same or similar questions. It is not necessary to reject Joshua's story or to read it against the backdrop of Jesus' teachings in order to find meaning in it. There is a self-critical feature of the text itself that must guide our interpretation.

PART ONE

God's Gift
of the Land

JOSHUA 1—12

Joshua 1—12, the first major division of the book, reports Israel's preparation to occupy Canaan (1:1—5:12) and the conquest of the land (5:13—12:24). At points these chapters are strikingly similar to other ancient Near Eastern battle reports, so much so that one suspects Joshua's authors were aware of and patterned chapters 1—12 after such extrabiblical texts (see the commentary on Joshua 3:1—5:1 and 5:13–15). Nevertheless, it is most important to notice that Joshua 1—12 is quite different from these parallel documents in some ways. Most important for our purposes, Joshua 1—12 draws attention to God as the primary actor, unlike the braggadocian royal recitals of Israel's neighbors, *told by kings* to garner political support. In other words, Joshua 1—12 focuses on God's grace, not on the political and military capability of a king or military general. It emphasizes that Canaan is God's gift to Israel, in fulfillment of divine promises to Abraham (Gen. 12:7; Josh. 1:3), and recognition of that fact is a primary tenet of faith. Hence, the story is punctuated, not by records of how many Canaanites were killed in battle or by details of Joshua's military strategy, but by accounts of Canaanites who were grafted into Israel because they acknowledged the power of the Lord (Josh. 2; 6:22–25; 9).

The fact that Joshua 1—12 is dominated by theological concerns should forewarn the reader that these chapters are not historical records in the modern sense. This point is borne out by comparing chapters 1—12 with the rest of Joshua and with Judges. The sweeping claims in Joshua 11:23 that "Joshua took the whole land" and "the land had rest from war" not only seem simplistic, but they do not square with material in other parts of Joshua. Indeed, Joshua 13—19, along with the book of Judges, portrays matters quite differently. It shows Israel living alongside other groups, giving sons and daughters to them in marriage, and sharing land and culture (Judg. 3:5). Most historians believe the delineation of early Israel in chapters 13—19 is closer to reality. Joshua 1—12 certainly has some historical roots, but this segment of the book is the product of theologians who collapsed varied and lengthy historical experiences into a story that first and foremost aims to make theological claims.

Joshua 1
Joshua's Installation

The beginning of a narrative often presents information that is necessary for understanding the rest of the story. Joshua 1 does this largely by connecting the reader to the values and theological ideals of Deuteronomy. It recalls that Joshua is Moses' successor, commissioned in Deuteronomy 31:23 and reaffirmed in Deuteronomy 34:9. Joshua 1 also points back to the instruction of Moses recorded in Deuteronomy, which, in written form, is now the primary authority for Joshua (Deut. 31:24–29; Josh. 1:7–8). In addition to the direct command to observe Moses' teachings, the language of Moses' torah appears in the chapter at every turn, creating further the impression that it is the standard by which Israel will be judged. Joshua 1 has the strong sense of Israel's unity that also appears in Deuteronomy. Following and referring to Moses' speech in Deuteronomy 3:18–22, Joshua orders the Reubenites, the Gadites, and the half-tribe of Manasseh to cross the Jordan armed with the other Israelites before returning to possess their territory east of the river (Josh. 1:12–18). Concern over these tribes and their territorial allotment will occur again in chapters 13 and 22. Hence, Joshua 1 prepares the reader for the remainder of the book by grounding the conquest and possession of the land in the theological interests of Deuteronomy.

"After the Death of Moses"

The first line of Joshua 1 sets Joshua's installation in the context of Moses' death (1:1; see 1:2). The words "after the death of Moses" connect the reader yet again to Deuteronomy by referring back to the report of Moses' death in Deuteronomy 34. But the death of Moses is more than a temporal marker. As Dennis Olson has observed, it is a very important theological theme in Deuteronomy that casts a shadow over all his speeches to Israel (Deut. 1:37; *Deuteronomy and the Death of Moses*, p. 18; see pp. 118–30, commentary on Josh. 24). The implications of Moses' death for Joshua 1 are at least three:

First, as Moses states in his opening address in Deuteronomy, his death divides Israel's early history into two distinct epochs of salvation (Deut. 1:37–38). The first period, which encompasses the exodus and wilderness wandering, is characterized by Israel's stubbornness and lack of faith. As a result, Moses and his entire generation will die out without entering the land of promise. The second epoch will be marked by the possession of the land through the leadership of Joshua. Hosea 12:13 may well have in mind this demarcation of generations and leaders: "By a prophet [Moses] the LORD brought Israel up from Egypt, and by a prophet [Joshua] he was guarded." Whether this is correct or not, Moses' death is clearly a watershed event because it creates this fissure in Israel's salvation history.

A second theological implication of Moses' death has to do with how Joshua succeeds Moses as God's prophet. Deuteronomy 34 says that Moses was unparalleled, that no one would match the wonders he worked for Israel or occupy his favored place as the one "whom the Lord knew face to face" (Deut. 34:10–12). This final evaluation of Moses creates tension with Deuteronomy 18:15–22, which says God will raise up a prophet like Moses after Moses' death. The implications of these two statements from Deuteronomy are played out in the person of Joshua. Joshua will speak as a prophet (Josh. 24:2), will intercede on Israel's behalf (Josh. 7:6–9), and will mediate the covenant (Josh. 8:30–35; 24), all in line with Moses' actions before him. And yet Joshua does not become Moses' equal, even though the Lord and Israel promise him their unqualified support (1:5, 17). Indeed, the titles for Joshua and Moses in Joshua 1:1 hint at a hierarchical relationship between the two. Moses is introduced as "the servant of the Lord," an epithet that recurs throughout the book to denote his unique place before God (the same label is given to David in 2 Sam. 3:18; 7:5). To be sure, this label is applied to Joshua in Joshua 24:29, as he mediates the covenant between God and Israel (see the commentary on chap. 24; compare Judg. 2:8), but in Joshua 1:1 Joshua is identified as "Moses' assistant." This title identifies him as Moses' disciple, one under Moses' authority, even as he is installed to take Moses' place.

Joshua is sometimes popularly described as a "second Moses," filling a role similar to that of Elisha in relation to Elijah. The Pseudepigraphical book of Pseudo-Philo draws this parallel. It says that Joshua received Moses' garments at Moses' death and was transformed by them, just as Elisha picked up Elijah's mantle in 2 Kings 2:13–14

21

(20:1–5; Pseudo-Philo is a Jewish work from the first century A.D; see Num. 20:25–28 for another possible inspiration for Pseudo-Philo's story). Nevertheless, the final evaluation of Moses in Deuteronomy 34:10–12 precludes a view of Joshua as Moses' equal. Joshua is presented, rather, as one endowed with "some" of Moses' authority, as Numbers 27:20 says.

The third, and most important, implication of Moses' death for the book of Joshua is that Moses' authority continues for Joshua through the written record of Moses' commands. In Deuteronomy, the emphasis on Moses' death serves to highlight the fact that Moses writes his torah and deposits it beside the ark of the covenant, which contained the "ten words" (Deut. 10:1–5; 31:24–29). In other words, all of Deuteronomy foreshadows that time when Moses' teachings in written form would become a surrogate for Moses himself. Joshua 1 shows the centrality of the law in explicit commands to keep Moses' teachings (Josh. 1:7–8), as well as in frequent citations and references to Moses' speeches. For example, much of the vocabulary in the Lord's charge to Joshua in Joshua 1:2–9 echoes Moses' orations in Deuteronomy 7:24; 11:24–25; 17:18–19. The Lord's specific promise that "no one will be able to stand against you" in Joshua 1:5 matches exactly the words of Moses in Deuteronomy 7:24 and 11:25. This shows that Moses' words are "canonical"; they are treated with the same seriousness as the word of the Lord and provide the primary benchmark for Joshua's leadership and for Israel's life in the land (Josh. 11:15, 23).

The Installation Service

The commissioning "ceremony" in Joshua 1:1–18 is much like the accounts of other well-known figures being appointed to specific tasks in the Old Testament (2 Chron. 19:4–11). These narratives typically contain (1) a charge of encouragement (in Joshua's case, the call to "Be strong and courageous"); (2) a description of mission (cross the Jordan; put Israel in possession of the land); and (3) a promise of assistance ("I will be with you"). But the story of Joshua's installation is most similar to the investiture of Solomon in 1 Kings 2:1–4. There David charges his son, much as the Lord enjoins Joshua in this chapter, "Be strong, be courageous" (1 Kgs. 2:2) and "keep the charge of the LORD your God . . . as it is written in the law of Moses" (1 Kgs. 2:3; McCarthy, "An Installation Genre?" p. 31). The use of this type of commissioning story probably indicates the author is trying to portray Joshua as a monarchical figure, like Josiah, the Judean king at the time much of Joshua was written. The royal character of Joshua becomes clear mainly in the content of Joshua's charge. The Lord commands Joshua to meditate on the book of the law, an ideal the king is expected to meet, according to Deuteronomy 17:19 (Josh. 1:8). The eastern tribes pledge their absolute loyalty, like an oath made by subjects to their monarch (Josh. 1:16–18). Furthermore, the singular "you" in verse 5 ("No one shall be able to stand against you") suggests that the military hopes of the entire people rest on the man Joshua, making him a figure akin to ancient Near Eastern kings who bore representative roles of leadership in battle.

Although Joshua 1 contains the typical features of an installation report, the unit as a whole does not divide neatly along lines created by these elements. Rather, it incorporates them (and they appear more than once) in a much fuller narrative that has three primary movements: (1) the Lord commissions Joshua (vv. 1–9); (2) Joshua addresses the people (vv. 10–11, 12–15); and (3) the people respond in obedience and support for Joshua (vv. 16–18).

The first two sections of the chapter contain two natural subdivisions. In section one (vv. 1–9) the Lord instructs Joshua to cross over the Jordan to capture the land (vv. 2–6) and to observe the torah of Moses (vv. 7–9). Similarly, in section two (vv. 10–15) Joshua addresses the people in two segments, divided according to two subgroups Joshua commands: Joshua directs the "officers of the people" to prepare to ford the Jordan in verse 11; in verses 12–15 Joshua directs the tribes that will settle east of the river first to cross with their kindred and assist in taking Canaan (vv. 1, 10, and 12 provide the settings of and introductions to the speeches).

The first segment of the two-part charge to Joshua (vv. 2–6) contains two imperatives: "proceed to cross the Jordan" (v. 2); "be strong and courageous" (v. 6). The commands are somewhat lost, however, amidst six promises of the Lord's action: "I have given," "as I promised," "shall be your territory," "no one shall be able to stand against you," "I will be with you," "I will not fail or forsake you." Such divine pledges highlight the power of God and render human action rather superfluous. This accent on divine action is evident particularly in the subjects and in the tenses of the verbs that follow the command to cross the Jordan. The first verb is a so-called imperfect, which may be translated either as future action ("your foot *will tread*"), as NRSV and NIV render, or as typical action ("your foot *happens to tread*"), as CEV chooses to express it. The Hebrew imperfect tense reflects the fact that the Israelites had not set foot in Canaan at the time of the Lord's speech to Joshua; any talk of their entry into the land is hypothetical. The second

23

verb, however, which has the Lord as its subject and is in the Hebrew perfect tense, is properly rendered as past action. NRSV expresses this in its translation, "I *have given* to you." NIV and CEV (and reflected in the Greek version), on the other hand, express the verb as an English future: "I *will give* to you." The choice of the future tense in these translations overlooks both the grammatical significance of the Hebrew perfect and the theological concern it carries. Namely, although the battle for Canaan had not begun, God had already determined that Israel would possess the land. The importance of the idea that Canaan is a gift is illustrated by the fact that the verbal root meaning "give" occurs eight times in this chapter, with either the Lord or Moses as its subject. The Israelites do have a role in "taking" the land (vv. 11 and 15), but their power is outweighed by God's grace. As we have already observed, this notion is a primary theme throughout the book (Josh. 2:9, 14, 24; 5:6; 8:1; 9:24; 13:6; 18:3; 22:4; 23:13, 15, 16; 24:13).

"Be strong and courageous" (v. 6a), the concluding imperative in this first part of the Lord's speech, appears also in the second charge (Josh. 1:7a, 9a) and again in the people's response to Joshua (Josh. 1:18b). These words are common in texts that give instructions for holy war (Deut. 3:28; 31:6,7; Josh. 10:25; 2 Chron. 32:7). In such contexts this so-called encouragement formula typically rests alongside statements concerning God's battle on behalf of Israel. Therefore, the words "be strong and courageous" are not really a call to be vigorous in waging war. Rather, they are primarily an injunction to trust and depend upon the Lord (Pss. 27:14; 31:24). The Israelites' reception of the land does not depend on human strength and courage; rather, the command to "be strong and courageous" calls for a particular response to God, who has already chosen to capture Canaan and to open it to the Israelites.

The central subject in this first segment of the Lord's address to Joshua is the acquisition of Canaan, but the text is unclear concerning the extent of the territory the Lord promised. Verse 4 is unique among biblical descriptions of the land. Deuteronomy 11:24 offers the most similar description, but Joshua 1:4 deviates from the Deuteronomy text in significant ways (cf. Gen. 15:18; Deut. 1:7). For instance, Deuteronomy 11:24 clearly lays out the expanse of a territory from south (the wilderness) to north (Lebanon) and from east (the great river) to west (the Great Sea), reflecting the farthest extent of the Davidic-Solomonic empire (2 Sam. 3:9–10; 24:1–9). To be sure, elements of Joshua 1:4 are parallel: "the Lebanon" clearly refers to the mountainous area that formed the united monarchy's northwestern border; from this boundary the land grant stretches to the Euphrates in the east; the Mediterranean Sea circumscribes the western limits of the territory. In contrast

24

to Deuteronomy 11:24, however, the present wording of Joshua 1:4 focuses the span on the northern part of the land, beginning and extending "from the wilderness and the Lebanon as far as the great river." In addition, Joshua's outline of the territory emphasizes an east-west axis, yet does not draw a cogent line from south to north, as does Deuteronomy 11:24. Furthermore, the meaning of the reference "from the wilderness" is unclear. Does the writer mean the eastern region from which the Israelites will enter the land or the southern desert (the Negev) as referred to in Genesis 15:18 in another outline of the land ("from the river of Egypt to the great river, the river Euphrates")? In addition to these differences between Joshua and other boundary lists, Joshua 1:4 uniquely names the territory to be captured as "all the land of the Hittites."

Some scholars explain the obfuscatory features of verse 4 as the result of scribal mistakes. They assume that Joshua 1:4 conformed originally to the pattern of Deuteronomy 11:24, but copyist errors, and subsequent attempts to correct them, resulted in a description of the land that differs in some significant ways from the Deuteronomy prototype. While this view may be correct, it does not help us to understand Joshua 1:4 as it now stands. What is clear is that Joshua's authors intended to make a magnificent claim in this verse about the territory to be captured now by the military prowess of the people empowered by the Lord. The reference to the Hittites encodes this message. Assyrian and Babylonian historical documents dating from about the time of Joshua's composition refer to the territory west of the Euphrates as the "land of the Hittites." The mention of the Hittites in these documents identifies the land with the powerful Anatolian kingdom that dominated much of the ancient Near East in the Late Bronze and Early Iron Ages (1550–900 B.C.). The Hittites rivaled the Egyptians, boasting a fierce fighting force that struck fear into the city-states and territories it attacked. By the time Joshua was written, this empire was in the dustbin of history, but the memory of it was so enduring that the territory was identified by the Hittite name. Joshua's original audience, perceiving the relationship in style between Joshua's land description and the battle accounts from Assyria and Babylon, likely sensed that Joshua's author was placing Israel in a category with these large, dominant empires of their day. Whatever the process of development, Joshua 1:4 aggrandizes Joshua's army as a dominant world power. This idealized portrait of Israel was meant to inspire a people and forge a grand faith that nothing was impossible with their God.

The second section of the Lord's oration to Joshua (vv. 7–9) begins and ends with the same injunction that appears in verse 6a:

25

"Be strong and very courageous." The use of these words in verse 7, however, is different from that in verse 6a. This time the imperatives are followed by an important purpose clause, "to act in accordance with all the law that my servant Moses commanded you." By these words the Lord galvanizes Joshua, making him "strong and courageous," not only in confidence concerning the Lord's promises (as in v. 6a), but also as a foundation for obedience. That is, the Lord instructs Joshua to be stout of heart *in order that* he may act according to Moses' words. The implications for the use of this phrase are profound. In the first set of instructions the Lord's charge to be strong and courageous intends to evoke faith that the land was a grant from God (vv. 2–6). Hence, where one expects a military commander to be given some concrete and measurable task (to take the land), his call is to believe in God's action. In the second segment of the address, the Lord indeed prods Joshua to particular action; yet his appointed deed is not conquest but obedience to divine law. To be sure, conquest and obedience are never fully separable in Joshua—the Israelite capture of Canaan is always judged by compliance with what "Moses the servant of the Lord commanded" (Josh. 11:12). Nevertheless, in the Lord's opening speech, obedience is clearly the consummate call to Joshua and the Israelites.

The phrase "this book of the law" identifies the object of Joshua's devotion as the set of precepts Moses first delivered to Israel on the plains of Moab. The "book" may be distinguished more exactly as the legislation in Deuteronomy 4:44—30:29. Deuteronomy 1:1—4:43 introduces the commands in these chapters, and Deuteronomy 31:9–13, 24–29 (cf. Deut. 27:3) makes provisions for their preservation, including the inscription of the words (Deut. 27:3; 31:9–13, 24–29) and their public reading.

At the center of the Lord's instructions concerning the Mosaic legislation are two commands to Joshua regarding the law: (1) "This book of the law shall not depart out of your mouth," and (2) "you shall meditate on it day and night." The first command posed a problem for some past interpreters; Calvin in particular wondered why God referred here to the mouth and not the eye, if the concern was for reading the text. He proposed that the mention of Joshua's mouth meant Joshua was charged with teaching the Mosaic law to the people (*Joshua,* p. 33). At the end of the book Joshua does inculcate the commands of Moses to Israel (Josh. 23:6–13); nevertheless, this is not the intention of the mouth reference in Joshua 1:7. The key to the meaning is in the parallel statement, "you shall meditate on it day and night." The expression "you shall meditate" denotes something akin to mumbling or speaking under the breath. Thus, it reflects the practice of reading aloud, which was common in the biblical world even when reading alone (Acts 8:30). Joshua's "meditation" is not casual (or quiet) reflection but active reading and study.

The "Book of the Law" and the Modern Reader

The second portion of the Lord's command to Joshua introduces what is arguably the central theological conviction in the book, the necessity of aligning self and community with the instructions of Moses (Deut. 5:32–33; 17:11, 19–20). Yet this theological interest puts many contemporary readers at odds with Joshua. Paul's words in Romans 7:6, "Now we are discharged from the law," have shaped the church's consciousness so that Christians often devalue the legal portion of Scripture, judging it to be passé, superceded by the revelation in Christ. Indeed, to speak of obedience to law seems to imply a works righteousness that the New Testament rejects (Rom. 4:13–15; Gal. 3:6–18). In defense of the law some have pointed out that the Hebrew term torah derives from a root with the broader meaning "instruction." Hence, the first five books of the Old Testament have come to be known as *the* torah; they house the codified stipulations in a larger narrative that recounts God's gracious election and salvation of Israel. As this reasoning goes, Christians can accept the torah as something that contains both law and "gospel"; law is embedded in the larger salvation story and offers a proper response to God's graciousness. But this perspective is of limited usefulness here, since torah in Joshua 1:7–8 does not refer to the whole Pentateuch, but more exclusively to the "statutes and ordinances" in Deuteronomy (Deut. 5:1). In other words, the term "law" in Joshua is used more narrowly, connoting Moses' Deuteronomic speeches that consist largely of legal codes.

Nevertheless, the church must not be too quick to dismiss Joshua's law as stale, legalistic, and confining. On the contrary, as Terence Fretheim has argued, the instructions of Moses in Deuteronomy all proceed from the first commandment and serve as specific illustrations of how one may show complete devotion to God (*Deuteronomic History*, pp. 23–24; see pp. 118–30, commentary on Josh. 24). In other words, the specific laws of Deuteronomy were not intended as an exhaustive list that Israel could first check, and then claim to have fulfilled their obligation to God. Rather, they provided a select register

27

of ways Israel could show its intention to love God alone and to be devoted to God with all their heart, soul, and might.

Moreover, when the laws in Deuteronomy are considered collectively, they are anything but legalistic and lifeless. Moses' injunctions together make up a kind of constitution that ensured equality and justice in Canaan. One of the clearest illustrations of this function of the Deuteronomic law is the instruction to the king in Deuteronomy 17:19 to read Moses' commands "all the days of his life, so that he may learn to fear the LORD his God." The intended impact of the torah upon the king is that he will view himself as any other Israelite, "neither exalting himself above other members of the community nor turning aside from the commandment, either to the right or to the left" (Deut. 17:20). Thus, the Mosaic torah is a call to justice towards other humans on the one hand and recognition of God as the ultimate ruler on the other hand. In other words, the Lord commands Joshua to meditate not on a lifeless legal code but on precepts that have the purpose of liberating the oppressed, ensuring justice for the weak, and forging an egalitarian society. The object of Joshua's attention is as dynamic and emancipating as the constitution of a democratic state, and indeed, Deuteronomy's law was intended to serve a similar purpose (McBride, "Polity of the Covenant People," pp. 229–44).

This emphasis on the law also raises a second objection, namely the notion that obedience to a body of legislation brings automatic success. In the first chapter the text twice declares that keeping the law brings prosperity:

> [D]o not turn aside from it to the right hand or to the left, so that you may be successful wherever you go. (v. 7)

> [Y]ou shall meditate on it day and night, so that you may be careful to act in accordance with all that is written in it. For then you shall make your way prosperous, and then you shall be successful. (v. 8)

Such statements may seem like expressions of an artless retribution theology that proposes a causal connection between obedience and material advantage. There are two problems with this interpretation, however. First, the command to obey torah and the attendant promises of success come only after declarations that the land has been given as a gift (1:3). Torah faithfulness is to be a response to, not a prerequisite for, God's grace (see the commentary on Josh. 23). Second, careful consideration of the biblical meaning of the expressions "make prosperous" and "be successful" makes a strict understanding of retribution unlikely here. The first of these words (Hebrew śakal, "to be successful") often

28

describes prudence and wisdom. The term appears, for example, in Psalm 2:10 in an admonition to the kings of the earth to "be wise" by submitting to the Lord and his anointed (see Pss. 14:2, 119:99; Prov. 1:3; 10:5; 14:35). "To prosper" (Hebrew *ṣalaḥ*) is similar. The phrase has to do with taking a path that is right, and the root word sometimes expresses "prosperity" as a figurative reference to right conduct (Ps. 37:7). Therefore, "to prosper" in the intended sense is to live in the knowledge of one's proper place before the creator. When God's sovereignty is duly acknowledged, the believer is set on a good path characterized by humility, compassion, and justice. Joshua declares that meditation on torah establishes such dependence on the Lord. This interrelationship of humility and ethical behavior compares very closely to Jesus' instructions concerning the hearing and doing of his words (Matt. 7:24–27; Luke 6:47–49). Those who hear the word properly will simultaneously be oriented properly to God and neighbor. Therefore, it is easy to see why Jesus did not reject the law as passé but, instead, held up injunctions from Deuteronomy as the highest and best instruction for humankind (Deut. 6:4–5; Matt. 22:36–40; Mark 12:28–34; Luke 10:25–28).

The Promise of Rest

Just as the Lord addresses Joshua twice, Joshua in turn offers two sets of instructions to the people. In both speeches to the Israelites the recurrent theme is the possession of the land that God pledged to the ancestors. The first and shortest message is addressed to the "officers of the people" (vv. 10–11). In this section, Joshua systematically hands down instructions for warfare. Terms like "officer" and "camp" assume a military setting. Moreover, the Hebrew term, *yaraš*, which appears twice in verse 11, may mean either "possess" or "dispossess," and it usually has the sense of taking something by force (Deut. 1:8, 21, 39). Despite the presence of military language and imagery, however, the overarching point is that the land is given, not taken. This does not mean that the conquest will be a peaceful, benign undertaking, but because the Lord provides the land, there will be no reason for Israel to boast over their own military capacity or success at making themselves secure. On the contrary, their greatest attention is to be to obedience and faith, not to military training or strategy.

The second portion of Joshua's oration is directed to the Reubenites, the Gadites, and the half-tribe of Manasseh (Josh. 1:12–15). Joshua repeats Moses' earlier promise that these Israelite tribes will settle east of the Jordan. Moses allotted the eastern territory to these two and a

29

half tribes, instructing them first to cross the Jordan and assist their fellow Israelites in the conquest of Canaan (Deut. 3:12–17, 18–22). Joshua 1:12–15 does the same. The repetitious affirmation of God's promise of rest and land creates yet another parallel between Moses and Joshua and between the books of Deuteronomy and Joshua. Joshua effectively summarizes and consistently follows Moses' command.

"Rest" is a central subject in Joshua's address to the eastern tribes that will arise again later in the book (21:44; 22:4). In Joshua 1:12–15 the term appears twice, in two slightly different forms: "The LORD your God is providing you a *place of rest*, and will give you this land" (Josh. 1:13b); " . . . until the LORD *gives rest* to your kindred as well as to you, and they too take possession of the land that the LORD your God is giving them" (Josh. 1:15a). The key term occurs first in a promise to the eastern tribes, and second in a statement about who will occupy the land west of the Jordan. "Rest" in both cases refers to life in the land in the absence of enemies, a central hope of the exodus (Exod. 33:14). Yet the full theological import of this theme can be appreciated only in light of the exilic setting of the final form of Joshua. If such talk of "rest" came from Israel as an occupying army or a conquering world power, their "rest" would result in the unrest of others who are dispossessed. Rest and the occupation of Canaan in Joshua 1:13 and 15, however, are a promise made in reality to a people themselves dispossessed by the Babylonian destruction of Jerusalem. This historical perspective of Joshua's audience is essential for the preacher. Reading Joshua 1 in its exilic context presses the church to understand "rest" as the result of rescue and healing after trauma and devastation. The preacher may find parallels to exilic Israel's desire for rest in the disruptions of divorce, bankruptcy, sickness, or the like. The meaning here is close to that in Reynolds Price's novel *The Promise of Rest*. The story centers on Wade Hutchinson, a young man from North Carolina, who now is estranged from his parents, lives in New York City, and suffers with AIDS. At his father's urging, he returns home for his last days. Wade's death brings relief from physical suffering and provides the context in which a broken family is healed. Application of the promises of rest in Joshua 1:13 and 15 should reflect such a situation of disorientation and promised comfort.

Hebrews 3:7—4:11 ties the promise of rest to the certainty of God's abiding peace and salvation. The author declares that ultimate rest was available for Israel from the beginning (Exod. 20:11), but the Israelites were deprived of rest because of their lack of faith (Ps. 95:11). Rest did not come in completeness through Joshua; thus David (in Ps. 95:11) declared that the chance for rest is still open. Hebrews recognizes this rest as a state entered by faith and characterized by grace from God through Christ.

Joshua 2
Rahab and the Israelite Spies

Joshua 2 is one of the richest and most intricately woven narratives in the book. It employs irony, humor, and folkloric qualities to create an irresistible plot in which a prostitute outsmarts two groups of men in order to preserve herself and her family during the Israelite attack on Jericho. The narrative has suspense, sexual innuendo, and an underdog who triumphs—everything a modern audience expects in a great story! Because of these features, Joshua 2 can and should be appreciated for its literary artistry. This chapter is also extremely important, however, for the theology of the book of Joshua.

Joshua 2 seems to have been inserted between two stories that once went together. Indeed, Joshua 3:2 uses the temporal reference "after three days" to show continuity with Joshua 1, which mentions the same time interval (see 1:11). It has been noted further that the spy mission in chapter 2 would have taken longer than the three days that passes between Joshua's installation and the Jordan crossing (and Josh. 2:22 says the spies stayed three days in the hills after leaving Rahab). Even if these references to "three days" are meant figuratively, the Rahab story still appears to interrupt the logical connection between chapters 1 and 3. The account's redactional location at the head of the conquest story, however, hints at its theological significance. The story highlights the question of how Israel will treat those living in the land. Specifically, the story alerts the reader that implementing the ban, the destruction of all the residents of Canaan, will be much more difficult and complex than the Deuteronomic law seems to indicate (Deut. 20:10–18). This tension is created as the character of Rahab invites admiration and sympathy. The favoritism towards her in turn shapes the presentation of the ban in chapter 6 and the remainder of the book.

Structure and Plot

As the story opens, Joshua commissions two spies, who travel to Jericho and lodge in Rahab's house (v. 1). The story has three main scenes, each of which features a conversation between Rahab and either

31

the Israelite spies or representatives of Jericho's king: (1) in verses 2–7 the king inquires through his emissaries as to the whereabouts of the spies; having hidden the men on her roof, Rahab gives false information that sends the king's posse on a wild goose chase; (2) verses 8–14 are set on Rahab's roof, where the men are concealed under a pile of flax; there Rahab strikes a bargain with the two spies, thus buying safety for herself and her household when the city is destroyed; (3) in verses 15–21 Rahab lowers the two Israelites from the city wall and gives them instructions for their escape; at that point the spies qualify their oath to Rahab; they demand that she place a crimson cord outside her window and keep her family within the house during the invasion; they make a parting request that she maintain absolute secrecy about the spy mission.

Sexual innuendo permeates the story and is a driving force in its plot. The name Rahab itself may be intended to evoke seductive and provocative images. The Semitic root, *rhb*, which means "to open" (giving rise to noun forms that mean "open place" or "broad place"), is used in Ugaritic epic material to refer to female genitalia. Likewise, the same term is often associated with sexual impropriety in the Old Testament (Isa. 57:8; Ezek.16:24, 31). This evidence leads Ellen Davis to suggest the name was "an old soldier's joke" ("Critical Traditioning," p. 743). That is, the appellation was humorously appropriate for the woman's profession, like naming an undertaker "Digger." Perhaps for this reason, the Babylonian Talmud says that the very mention of Rahab's name could cause the speaker to be aroused sexually (tractate Megillah 15a). However, if this association with Rahab's name is accurate, the humor is ironic. As Davis also points out, Rahab is not the "broad" suggested by her name; rather, she is the most savvy character in the story. She thwarts the efforts of the king to capture the spies, and she maneuvers the spies into an oath that will protect her and her family. Moreover, of all the characters in Joshua 2, Rahab is the most keenly aware of the Lord's sovereignty, and she confesses that knowledge in classic Deuteronomic language.

Although the significance of Rahab's name and its possible association with prostitution are not certain, clear allusions to sexual activity help drive the narrative. In the opening verse, the expressions "entered" (literally "came into") and "spent the night" (literally "lay down"), which are sometimes used as circumlocutions for sexual intercourse, hint at an intimate affair between Rahab and the Israelite spies. In actuality, verse 1 states only that the scouts entered Rahab's house (compare Judg. 16:1), creating ambiguity about whether or not they became Rahab's customers. What is clear is that Rahab leads the king's representatives to believe they were her clients, thus gaining an advantage over the king.

She declares to the king's men, "True, the men came to me, but I did not know where they came from" (v. 4b). The implication of her statement is that she did not concern herself with their business in the city, only with their business with her. All the while, the reader is aware that Rahab has hidden the men and that her report of the men leaving is a lie (v. 5a). Furthermore, her suggestion, "Pursue them quickly, for you can overtake them," is disingenuous (v. 5b). Rahab effectively uses her role as prostitute to cover the fact that she is harboring the spies.

Later interpreters, uncomfortable with Rahab's identity as a prostitute, tried to tone down the offense of her profession, calling her a landlord (the Aramaic version or Targum), an innkeeper (Josephus, *Antiquities of the Jews* 5.1.2), or a "dealer of goods" (the medieval exegete Rashi used the similarity of the words "prostitute," Hebrew *zonah*, and "wares," *zwn*, to give this interpretation). But there is no hint of such discomfort in Joshua 2. The only question one might ask concerning the presentation of Rahab in Joshua 2 is, "What type of prostitute was she?" How one answers this question determines the overall interpretation of the story. For example, if Rahab was a cult prostitute, who offered sexual activity as part of a system of worship meant to encourage a pagan deity to fertilize the ground, then the story portrays a contest to name the true God of heaven and earth. Following this idea, some have suggested Rahab was a moon-priestess, and that she used her rooftop as a cult site, with the flax that covered the spies doubling as objects to facilitate pagan worship. Given such a scenario, Rahab's confession of faith is a capitulation of the land to the Lord as the superior deity (Noort, *Das Buch Josua*, p. 133).

While the interpretation is interesting and would give a dramatic cast to Rahab's confession of the Lord's power, there is no indication in the text that the stalks of flax are anything more than raw materials from which linen will be made. The rooftop was a propitious place to allow dew to soak the plants as preparation to spread their fibers. Moreover, the typical term for cult prostitute is not used here (*qedešah*; see Deut. 23:18; Hos. 4:14). Instead the word is a more general term that refers to one who commits fornication (*zonah*; cf. Judg. 19:2). Although the term is paired with the word for sacred prostitute in Hosea 4:14 and Genesis 38:21–22, 24, it appears alone in Joshua 2:1, and there is no indication that her activity has religious overtones. She is most likely a common prostitute, who was perhaps forced into her profession to pay family debts. In other words, Rahab was the victim of an economic system in which women had no opportunities to earn a living; women like her sometimes found themselves on the edge of life, with slavery or prostitution their only options. If that is the assumption of the story's author and audience, then Rahab's role as prostitute may actually foster sympathy for her.

After Rahab's conversation with the members of the king's posse and their departure, the scene closes with the terse comment, "As soon as the pursuers had gone out, the gate was shut" (v. 7b). The closed gate is significant for the next scene, because it means that, in effect, the spies are now trapped in the city, at the mercy of the woman who has just saved them. This part of the story has touches of irony. On the surface, Rahab's confession and subsequent request that they spare her life seem to indicate her dependence on the spies. In the larger story she is dependent on them, but on her rooftop, beneath a pile of flax, in a place where their movement might be detected by Rahab's neighbors, the spies are at Rahab's mercy. Rahab simultaneously saved the men of Israel from their pursuers and bound them to an oath to save her. The men show they recognize her advantage over them when they say, "Your life for ours." This transposition of power appears again when the Israelites qualify their vow from outside the city wall. Only when Rahab releases the men from the rooftop hideout do they feel free to negotiate with her. By the time they set their conditions, however, Rahab's primary request has already been granted on oath (Nelson, *Joshua*, pp. 49–52). Hence, the story's internal movement features this woman's wisdom in dealing with a crisis for herself and her family.

When verse 15a says, "Then she let them down by a rope through the window," the reader may remember the gate of the city was already shut (v. 7) and wonder what good this would do the spies. Perhaps to account for this question, the Hebrew text includes a comment not found in the Greek version: "for her house was on the outer side of the city wall and she resided within the wall itself" (v. 15b). The explanation refers to a casemate structure consisting of two parallel walls, the double-wall adding security to the city's defensive system. Archaeologists have discovered the space between such walls sometimes filled with rubble but at other times partitioned for storage or to provide dwelling space. This is the type of living quarters Joshua 2:15b describes for Rahab. The explanation in verse 15 clarifies how the woman both trapped the spies in the city and then released them from the city after their oath.

Rahab's Confession (2:9–13)

At the heart of the second scene in the story (vv. 8–14) is a bold speech (vv. 9–13) in which Rahab pays tribute to Israel's God. To be sure, her oration serves largely to explain the risk she has taken to protect the two spies and to bargain for her life. Nevertheless, the words of this foreign woman are striking in the way they attest to the power and identity of the Lord. Her discourse consists of two parts: in verses 9–11 Rahab makes a confident statement of faith; and in verses 12–13 she pleads for safety for herself and her family when the city is attacked.

The confessional portion of Rahab's speech (vv. 9–11) has two sub-sections. The first segment (v. 9), built upon Rahab's opening declaration, "I know," concerns the Canaanites' fearful reaction to the Israelite entry into the land. Then the content of what she "knows" about the inhabitants' state of mind is presented in three consecutive and similarly structured lines in verse 9, each introduced by the same Hebrew particle (*ki*), usually translated "for," "because," or "that." This gives a certain cadence and structure to Rahab's statement: "I know *that* the Lord has given you the land, and *that* dread of you has fallen on us, and *that* all the inhabitants of the land melt in fear before you."

The second portion of the confession (vv. 10–11) is also ordered by a prominent verb, "we heard," that appears at the beginning of both verses. Moreover, these verses begin and end with lines introduced by the same Hebrew particle that dominates verse 9. This little word in verses 10 and 11 is probably intended as an intensive marker; therefore, it may be appropriate to translate it differently from most English translations at points: "*Indeed*, we heard . . ." (v. 10a); " . . . indeed, the LORD your God is God in heaven above and on earth below" (v. 11b). Verse 10 contains a concatenation of clauses that makes emphatic Rahab's awareness of the Lord's power and control over Canaan. The rhetorical force comes by Rahab expressing what she heard in three similarly structured clauses, each introduced by "how" or "what": "*how* the LORD dried up the water of the Red Sea before you when you came out of Egypt" (v. 10a); "*what* you did to the two kings of the Amorites that were beyond the Jordan" (v. 10bα); "*how* you put them (the Amorite kings) under the ban" (v. 10bβ; NRSV: "whom you utterly destroyed").

In the second major section of her speech (vv. 12–13) Rahab seeks a pledge from the Israelite spies to return her kindness by keeping her and her family safe. The key term here, the Hebrew word *ḥesed*, is used in the Old Testament to denote the faithfulness expected in a covenant relationship, the type of faithfulness God showed to Israel. Rahab argues that her *ḥesed* towards the spies (v. 12a) should require Israel likewise to act with faithfulness towards her and the members of her household (vv. 12b-13).

Joshua 2:9–11 has many connections to the various literary strands or sources that constitute Genesis through Deuteronomy, making this text a battlefield for scholars who want to show a primary connection to either Genesis through Numbers (and see Joshua as originally part of a

Hexateuch), or to Deuteronomy (understanding the book as originally part of the Deuteronomistic History). Without doubt much of Rahab's speech does employ Deuteronomic language, so that this foreign woman expresses the essence of Deuteronomic theology. For example, Rahab's opening comment, "the Lord has given you the land," parallels the Lord's promise to Joshua in Joshua 1:2 and Moses' words in Deuteronomy 1:21. Thus, in good Deuteronomic parlance, Rahab acknowledges that Israel's God is the true owner of the land and has chosen to assign the territory to Israel. Much of the rest of Rahab's speech also draws its vocabulary from Deuteronomy. Her reference to the Canaanites melting in fear is reminiscent of Moses' recollection of his people's response to their spies' report (Josh. 2:9, 11; Deut. 1:28) and confirms Moses' prediction that the Canaanites would have "dread and fear" because Israel entered the land (Deut. 2:25). When Rahab speaks of the two Amorite kings, Sihon and Og, being defeated by the Israelites, she raises a subject that serves as part of the temporal setting for Moses' first speech in Deuteronomy (Deut. 1:4) and constitutes a significant part of that speech (see also Num. 21:21–35). In this portion of her confession Rahab says Israel "utterly destroyed" Sihon and Og (Josh. 2:10). Here she uses a verbal form of a Hebrew root (ḥrm) meaning "to devote to destruction" or "to place under the ban." The term refers to the practice of annihilating all the residents of Canaan in cities Israel will occupy (Deut. 20:10–20). In her dealings with the spies Rahab seeks an exemption from this practice.

Rahab's confession in Joshua 2:9–11 makes it tempting to conclude that she converted to Israelite faith and became a full member of the covenant community. Many Jewish and Christian interpreters have certainly read the story that way. In rabbinical tradition Rahab married Joshua and seven kings and eight prophets came from her lineage (see references in Ginsberg, *The Legends of the Jews*, 4:5; 6:171). Similarly, Matthew 1:5 names Rahab as the mother of Boaz and, hence, an ancestor of Jesus. The text itself never actually says that she devoted herself to the Lord. She refers to the Lord as "your God." This might indicate that her confession was based on an objective observation of God's power over other gods but not a subjective identification with the Lord (Josh. 2:11b). Nevertheless, Rahab does recognize Israel's God as the universal sovereign, the one who is in control of all territory and who has power to allot it to whomever he chooses. Whether or not she identifies personally with Israel's God is not as important in the story as the fact that she properly identifies the Lord as the power to whom she should bow. This recognition sets her apart from all other Canaanites except the residents of Gibeon (Josh. 9). Indeed, Rahab's speech fol-

36

lows a pattern that is replicated in Joshua 5:1; 9:1–2; 10:1–5; and 11:1–5. In each of these cases it is said that the residents of the land "heard" what the Lord did for Israel or what Israel did through the Lord's empowerment, and they responded either fearfully or antagonistically. Rahab and the Gibeonites both declare that they "heard" specifically what the Lord did to the Egyptians and how the Lord conquered Sihon and Og for Israel (Josh. 2:10; 9:9–10). Their response to this information distinguishes them from the other Canaanites by their attempts to make covenants with the invaders (see Stone, "Ethical and Apologetic Tendencies," pp. 25–36).

In light of these observations, it is not clear that the oration Rahab offers in 2:9–11 is intended to portray this Canaanite woman as a proselyte in the strict sense of the word. What is certain is that the speech contributes to the characterization of the harlot as one who is shrewd and discerning. In contrast to the king of Jericho and all the other Canaanites except the residents of Gibeon, she immediately perceives the Israelite threat and capitulates to the power of Israel's God. Rahab's confession also serves to speak beyond the characters in the story to a reader who knows the book of Deuteronomy. Indeed, the author of Joshua used Rahab's voice to remind the reader of God's earlier promises about life in the promised land (Deut. 1:21; Josh. 1:2) and to offer proof that those earlier promises were in effect.

Rahab's Crimson Cord (2:15–21)

Adding to the richness and complexity of the Rahab story is the mention of a crimson cord that the spies order Rahab to tie in her window, presumably to identify her home for preservation. Jewish tradition correlates the reddish color of Rahab's cord with blood placed on doorposts and lintels to protect the Israelites from the death angel on the night of the first passover (Exod. 12:7). Similarly, many Christian interpreters have seen the object as a symbol of the blood of Christ (Spurgeon, *The Treasury of the Bible*, 1:510). The association with Christ's blood is obviously a later interpretation that the story's authors did not intend. Certain features of the narrative, however, suggest a link with passover and exodus. Namely, the particular color placed outside the window is broadly similar to the blood on the portals in Egypt, and the spies' order for Rahab to keep her family members inside the house during the attack parallels Israel's practice on the night the death angel passed over (Exod. 12:22). But did Joshua's authors intend such a symbolic meaning? To answer the question with certainty is neither possible nor necessary. The tradition of interpreting Joshua 2 allegorically

37

itself is important, and it would be a mistake to think the only "right" interpretation is one that places the reader solidly within the mind of the text's author. The question of the author's intentions is important, however, because it helps us understand features of the text that were meaningful to the earliest audience. That is, without searching for the author's intentions, some of the story's potential meaning may be missed by our moving too quickly to later interpretations.

Several points about the crimson cord must be clarified. The first questions that must be answered concern the object itself: What does "cord" mean? Was it already in Rahab's house, or did the spies give it to her? Since the Israelite spies speak of it as an object before them (*"this* crimson cord"), and since they make their statement after being dropped from Rahab's window, it is tempting to understand the cord as the line Rahab used to lower them to safety (see v. 18). Nevertheless, this does not seem to be the intention of the story. Hebrew has a word meaning "rope" that appears in verse 15 to describe the means by which Rahab let the spies down from her window. Although the reference in verse 15 may be an explanatory addition to the text, as some scholars suggest, those who added the comment chose a word different from the term meaning "cord" that appears in verses 18 and 21.

The expression "crimson cord" in Hebrew is actually three words that stand in relationship to each other, including the word denoting the color crimson. The word translated "cord" is *tiqwah*, which comes from a verbal root meaning "to be tense/rigid" and, by extension, "to be expectant." The noun form elsewhere in the Old Testament has the second connotation and means "hope." A related form (*qaw*), which appears numerous times, always refers to a measuring line, as used in construction (1 Kgs. 7:23; Job 38:5). If this related term is any clue, it would further argue against the idea that *tiqwah* refers to a rope. The second word in the expression "crimson cord" is the Hebrew *ḥût*, meaning "thread." Hence, although English translations do not show it, the two words together have the sense of a "cord of thread." Again, this seems to refer to a line not substantial enough to support the Israelite spies (see the use of *ḥût*, "thread" in Judg. 16:12; Eccl. 4:12).

Although it is not certain, the "cord of thread" probably refers to a strand of material from which cloth would be woven. That it was a crimson cord, not a whole piece of cloth, makes sense when we realize that ancient Near Eastern people typically dyed individual strands so that the cords might then be woven together with others of different colors to make cloth (Albright, *The Excavation of Tell Beit Mirsim*, 3:60–61).

As to the question of the origin of the crimson cord, again there is uncertainty. It should be noted, however, that Rahab does not tie the cord in her window until verse 21, after the spies depart. Hence, "this crimson cord" likely refers to an object that the spies see in the house, a point that is supported further by the discussion below. The fact that the spies' demand concerning the thread comes after they have been lowered from the house does create difficulty for the reader, but it probably indicates that the author, at that point, is reverting back to the previous scene.

If the crimson cord is not the rope that lowered the spies to the ground, but a common piece of material that Rahab had on hand, it suggests an interesting portrait of Rahab and her house. The cord, along with the flax on the roof, shows that Rahab's house was more than a brothel. It contained a private industry by which Rahab clothed members of her household. With these elements in her home, Rahab the harlot is amazingly like the virtuous woman in Proverbs 31:10–31! Indeed, Proverbs praises this woman particularly for dressing her family in crimson (Prov. 31:21) and for working with flax (Prov. 31:13). These parallels between Rahab and the ideal wife of Proverbs are at least heuristically useful in the interpretation of Joshua 2, if not reflective of the author's intended portrait of the harlot. The larger delineation of Rahab, as of the wife in Proverbs 31:10–31, is of a woman who went to great lengths to care for her family. Both women were exemplary in their fulfillment of familial obligations, albeit in radically different circumstances. In Rahab's case, the identity as a prostitute might even be part of this larger picture of model behavior, if her harlotry was a means of satisfying family debts. Regardless, Rahab expresses faithfulness in part through deception and cunning that allowed the family to be preserved. This characterization of disreputable activity as "faithfulness" may seem strange to contemporary readers, regardless of what motivated the actions. To understand Rahab in her own context, however, and to see her as related in character to the woman in Proverbs 31, one must imagine a world in which the highest obligation for a woman was to fulfill commitments to husband, father, and children. In such a world, a woman like Tamar could be called "righteous" after posing as a cult prostitute and becoming pregnant by her father-in-law, because these extreme measures fulfilled her obligations under the law of levirate marriage (Gen. 38:26; Deut. 25:5–10; note also that crimson thread is part of Tamar's story; see Gen. 38:28). With such a world in view, Rahab's crimson cord, along with the flax on her roof, indeed suggests that her character is at the core the same as that of the ideal wife in Proverbs 31:10–31. Therefore, if Rahab's crimson cord is a symbol of hope, like the blood on the doorposts and lintels in the exodus story, it is hope forged from Rahab's constant care for her family. She shows herself a woman of worth by doing whatever it takes to preserve them.

Genre and Purpose of the Story

What is the purpose of the story in Joshua 2? The method of study known as form criticism has taught us that a text's genre, or literary type, largely determines that text's purpose or what it intends to communicate. In the case of Joshua 2, the problem of genre is particularly acute. Some scholars have labeled the account a spy story, indicating that it is principally about a reconnaissance mission. Others have identified Joshua 2 as an etiology, that is, as a story meant to explain some reality that existed at the time of the writing; in this case, the story would explain why Rahab's descendents continued to live among the Israelites, even though Moses commanded Israel to annihilate the residents of Canaan (Deut. 20:10–20). Still others have seen in the Rahab story a tale of hospitality; foreigners are taken in and protected by a local resident, just as Lot housed the divine visitors in Genesis 19 and an old man in Judges 19 welcomed a Levite and his concubine. Features of all these story types are present in Joshua 2, but the story is not dominated by any one of them. It is likely that the account developed and changed over time, with different emphases predominating at different stages of growth. Nevertheless, the present narrative and its setting in Joshua give us some clues as to how we ought to read Joshua 2 as part of the book.

A casual reading of Joshua 2 might give the impression that the story is indeed primarily about a spy mission. The account begins with Joshua sending two spies to "view the land, especially Jericho" (2:1), and concludes with the spies' report when the mission is complete (2:24). Moreover, Joshua 2 has features that recall the story of Moses sending spies. Joshua's starting point in Shittim is the same as Moses' in Numbers 13:1; the term in Joshua 2:2 translated "search out" is found only here and in Moses' speech about his spy mission in Deuteronomy 1:22. Hence, the story is about two Israelite spies and intentionally recalls the best-known Old Testament spy narrative, thus linking Joshua to Moses in his giving orders to search out the land.

A closer reading of Joshua 2, however, raises doubts about whether the story is primarily a spy account. The spies hardly "view the land"; they view only the inside of Rahab's house and her rooftop. Moreover, the report they bring back to Joshua can scarcely be termed "intelligence." They report only what Rahab told them (2:9–11), which the Lord had already proclaimed to Joshua (Josh. 1:2–3) and Moses promised all Israel (Deut. 2:25). In addition, if Joshua 2 was intended to be a story of scouting Canaan that draws parallels between Moses and Joshua, why is Joshua's act not condemned? After all, Moses' spy mission was interpreted as a sign of faithlessness that prevented him and his generation from entering the land (Deut. 1:22–40).

In fact, the story does not focus on Joshua sending spies or on hospitality, even though it contains both of these themes. Joshua 2 does have a clear etiological purpose. It helps explain why Rahab's people continued to live among the Israelites when Israel had been commanded to obliterate all the indigenous population (Deut. 20:10–20). The etiological ending to the story comes at the conclusion of the account of the capture of Jericho:

> But Rahab the prostitute, with her family and all who belonged to her, Joshua spared. Her family has lived in Israel ever since. For she hid the messengers whom Joshua sent to spy out Jericho. (Josh. 6:25)

Nevertheless, the story's greatest impact on the book, and its primary purpose, is not etiological so much as it is theological. The account raises for the first time in the book the issue of the ban (Josh. 2:10b) and, more specifically, the question of how Joshua's army will implement it. The issue sets Joshua 2 in an important relationship with Joshua 1. The first chapter of the book presented the Mosaic law as the benchmark by which Joshua's leadership will be judged. Now Joshua 2 zeroes in on this one tenet of Moses' torah that will provide the primary test case in the book of Joshua.

Joshua 2 and the Ethics of Violence

If the purpose of Joshua 2 is to introduce the problem of the ban, this story and its conclusion in Joshua 6 have important implications for how we relate the book of Joshua to the issues of violence and warfare. Christian ideals almost require a rejection of the assumption that God literally fought for Israel and commanded Israel to annihilate the Canaanites. This has led many Christian scholars to view Joshua in one of three ways, none of which removes the offense of divinely sponsored violence. (1) Some, like Calvin, guided primarily by the doctrine of divine sovereignty, argue that the Canaanites were rightly the object of God's wrath because they were so depraved, as Deuteronomy 9:5 indicates (Calvin, *Joshua*, p. 97). This explanation satisfies few modern readers. (2) Therefore, more recently it has been suggested that the book of Joshua came early in Israelite thinking about God's relationship to the nations; later in Israel's history the violence of holy war was spiritualized, that is, God's warfare became a battle against the forces of evil, not against real flesh-and-blood enemies. This approach to the problem does show that the Old Testament as a whole is not dominated

41

by divine sanction of physical violence; nevertheless, such a perspective leaves the impression that Joshua is a brutish book that is unredeemable apart from the later tradition that repudiates its claims. (3) Another way of dealing with the problem is to argue for the historical inaccuracy of Joshua's conquest story. Some archaeological evidence and sociological analysis seems to support the notion that Israel possessed Canaan through a gradual infiltration of the land. Some would suggest that the "conquest" was actually a rebellion of people already living in the land against oppressive overlords (see the commentary on Josh. 10—12). Thus, as the story was told, the oppressors were "written in" as Canaanites, and the righteous peasants in the revolt became Israel. If one of these theories is correct (and the evidence is not conclusive), it removes the problem of violence from Israel's history, or it makes it more acceptable as revolt against injustice, though the problem remains in the text.

The common failing of all three of these approaches is that they give insufficient credit to the authors of Joshua for their sensitivity to the problem of violence. As Lawson Stone summarizes,

> They all assume the text of Joshua unreservedly endorses Israel's extermination of the Canaanites, that the ancient writers cared little for the ethical question and therefore that the contemporary reader must look beyond or beneath the text for assistance. ("Ethical and Apologetic Tendencies," p. 27)

Stone argues further that these approaches have overlooked signs that indicate Joshua's authors were themselves uneasy about their own tradition of Canaanite depravity and Israelite conquest. The story of Rahab is the first of many prominent signs of that theological inquietude. As we have already noted, Rahab's speech, in which she confesses knowledge of the power of Israel's God, sets her apart from her Canaanite brethren and leads to her salvation. Granted, the other residents of Jericho will be slain in Israel's attack (Josh. 6), but Rahab's preservation establishes an interesting pattern in the conquest story. Far from confirming the Deuteronomic claim (Deut. 9:4–5) that the nations in the land are reprehensible, the Rahab story illustrates the reverse. As Ellen Davis observes, "In the story of Rahab, the stock notion of Canaanite wickedness is ironized and radically relativized, if not demolished altogether" ("Critical Traditioning," p. 742). Although the problem of the Canaanites and their destruction is not dissolved, it is tempered by the fact that all the Canaanites who are not faceless are theologically perceptive; they acknowledge the Lord as the universal sovereign, and are saved as a result. Rahab's speech, and the way it precipitates salvation for her and her family, gives the impression that any Canaanite who surrendered to Israel's God could be saved. That is precisely the way a strand of rabbinic tradition understood the matter. In an interpretation of Joshua 11:19 ("There was not a town that made peace with the Israelites") the Jerusalem Talmud, Tractate Sheviit 10.1 (16b) reasons that all the Canaanites were given opportunity to make peace, but they refused (Hoffman, "The Deuteronomistic Concept of Herem," p. 197; see pp. 89–96, commentary on Josh. 10—12). The presence of the Rahab story at the beginning of the conquest indicates that Joshua's authors also thought that there was hope for the Canaanites.

At the same time the Canaanites are elevated in their theological acceptability, the Israelites in Joshua 2 are, if anything, presented as disloyal to God and undeserving of God's miraculous acts. It is certainly possible to read the whole spy story as a sign of Israel's lack of faith, since Israel had been boldly charged to enter the land with assurance of success (Josh. 1:6, 7, 18). Even if this is not the intent of Joshua 2, it is striking that the only sins reported in Canaan are those of Israel (see Davis, "Critical Traditioning," p. 742). As Robert Polzin further proposes, this inversion of expectations concerning righteousness and wickedness produces a unique view of Rahab as representative of both Israel and the nations in the land:

> The underlying ideological position of the Rahab story as a preview of the entire book of Joshua is that some nations (represented by Rahab) will be spared a punishment they deserve, just as Israel (also represented by Rahab) obtains a land they do not deserve. (*Moses and the Deuteronomist*, p. 90)

This type of ironic reversal at work in the story of Rahab does not remove the problem of the ban from the book of Joshua. It does show, however, that the authors of the story themselves were concerned at least to demonstrate that Israel's God did not sponsor wholesale slaughter of Canaanites; those who professed faith in the Lord *could* be saved. As we shall see, this type of critical reflection on the tradition of the ban will recur each time the problem of the Canaanites and their annihilation is raised in the book.

Joshua 3:1—5:1

Crossing the Jordan

The crossing of the Jordan is remembered as one of the key events in Israel's history. Just as the Red Sea miracle changed Israel's status from slave to free, so Joshua 3:1—5:1 says the trek through the Jordan transformed Israel from a wandering band to a landed people, a nation. The event became deeply symbolic within the biblical period, as evinced by the story of Elisha striking the Jordan with Elijah's mantle, thus parting the waters, and passing over the riverbed into a new role as God's prophet (2 Kgs. 2:13–14). Later Jewish and Christian literature abounds with examples of the story's influence: *4 Ezra* speaks of God dividing the Euphrates to aid the northern Israelite exiles on their way to Assyria (13:44); Christian hymns such as "Guide Me, O thou Great Jehovah" speak of the Jordan as the passageway into eternal life.

Despite the significant impact of this story on Jewish and Christian tradition, several of its features create great difficulty for the reader. Although the Jordan crossing and its significance are obviously the main subjects of the story, the account is filled with other topics that compete for the reader's attention: the sacred nature of the ark and the priesthood, the unity of Israel, and the exaltation of Joshua. In addition to these multiple topics crowded together in the story, Joshua 3:1—5:1 has side comments and a frequent overlapping of action that draw the reader's attention away from the flow of the narrative (for a detailed discussion of the problem, see Hawk, *Joshua*, pp. 54–55). Therefore, the interpretation of this text has often turned into an attempt to sort out the literary strands that make up the story or to reconstruct the editorial process that produced the present complex account. Such efforts, though understandable, have not produced a satisfactory solution to the quandary of the narrative's development.

Our task is not to solve these problems but to make sense of the story as it now stands. The primary barrier to such analysis is the crowded details of the account, which make it nearly impossible to follow a consistent plot line. But the difficulty is alleviated when we realize that the story's intentions are to instruct, not to entertain. Indeed, there are at least two indications that the text has teaching as a primary goal.

First, chapter 4 is anchored by two subunits that inculcate the significance of the Jordan crossing and instruct Israel in how to remember it (4:1–7, 19–24; see Butler, *Joshua*, p. 42). In both cases, a child's question, "What do these stones mean (to you)?" (vv. 6, 21), prompts an explanation of the meaning of the event. Structurally these sections are much like the modern catechism. It is easy to see that the story's attempt to instruct is primary and overrides its effort to report.

Second, the entire event is presented as an elaborate ritual. The people prepare for it as for a holy act. Indeed, the term translated "sanctify" in Joshua 3:5 refers to a purification process like that which priests undergo before entering the sanctuary or handling sacred objects (Exod. 19:22; 1 Chron. 15:12). The ritual character of Joshua 3:1—5:1

is so pronounced that Frank Cross suggests this account was inspired, not by Israel's first fording of the Jordan, but by a later ceremonial crossing of the river at a spot that had been dammed for that purpose. Cross thinks the purpose of the ceremony was to re-create the parting of the Red Sea in a cultic drama at the Jordan. His theory makes sense insofar as Joshua 3:1—5:1 itself is aware of the symbolic nature of the Jordan crossing and states that this event should remind the audience of the Red Sea miracle. This is most evident in the way Joshua 3:1—5:1 uses language from the exodus story. Joshua 3:13 predicts that the waters of the Jordan, like the Red Sea, "shall be cut off; they shall stand in a single heap" (see 3:14–17), the word for "heap" being the same term that appears in Exodus 15:8. Numerous other references are similar (compare Josh. 4:19–24 with Exod. 14:21, 22, 29). Nevertheless, Cross must emend Joshua 3:13 to make his theory work. He argues the expression "single heap" was added by a later editor for ease of reading, and that originally the text simply referred to the river "standing," a reference to being stopped up or dammed (*Canaanite Myth and Hebrew Epic*, p. 138). Whether or not the event was ever dramatically enacted in the way Cross envisions, and whether or not the present story was generated by such a ceremony at the Jordan, it is clear that the event as presented is overlaid with interpretation and cast in liturgical form. In other words, Joshua 3:1—5:1 was shaped for the purpose of creating a proper memory of the Jordan crossing and instructing each generation as to its importance in Israelite history.

Our analysis of this section of the book will attempt to follow the instructional character of the narrative so as to answer the question, "What does this story intend to teach?" But first we will discuss the larger literary context of Joshua 3:1—5:1 and the overarching movement of the unit.

Literary Features

Even though it is nearly impossible to discern a consistent plot in Joshua 3:1—5:1, the story does have a measure of unity, as well as a certain logic that should be recognized. The account presents itself as part of the larger story that began in chapters 1 and 2. The reference to Shittim (3:1) as a starting point indicates a geographical setting at the same base camp from which Joshua sent spies (2:1). Also, Joshua 3:2 states that the Jordan crossing takes place "after three days," a note that puts the event in the time frame Joshua laid out in 1:11, with the scouting mission of chapter 2 filling the three-day interval. To be sure, a scouting expedition like that described in Joshua 2 would have required more

45

than three days. But the "three day" references are figurative, denoting a brief time of uncertain length, as evinced by the similar use of the phrase in Joshua 9:16. The figurative sense of "three days" appears in the New Testament, in predictions of Jesus being raised "after three days" in Mark's Gospel as well as in temporal notes in Acts 25:1; 28:7, 12, and 17 (see Mark 8:31; note how Matthew changes the reference to "*on* the third day" to be more exact; see Matt. 16:21).

Thematically, the variegated material in Joshua 3:1—5:1 is held together by two features of the story. First, twenty-one occurrences of the Hebrew verb *'abar*, meaning "to cross over" or "to traverse," communicate the primary subject of the narrative. The story begins with a series of preparatory speeches (Josh. 3:2–13) by the "officers" (vv. 2–4), Joshua (v. 5–6a, 9–13), and the Lord (vv. 7–8), and then the Israelites cross the Jordan. The Israelites create a memorial to the event at the place where the ark effected the river's stoppage. Then the story closes with a report of the Canaanite reaction to the miraculous occurrence (5:1). At every turn the mention of "crossing over" keeps the reader in touch with the main subject. Second, additional cohesion is provided by patterns of command/obedience and prediction/fulfillment (Hawk, *Joshua*, pp. 60–61; Nelson, *Joshua*, p. 58). For example, the Lord promises to exalt Joshua in 3:7, and 4:14 records this as a reality; in 3:13 Joshua says the waters of the Jordan will stand in a single heap, and in 3:16 this takes place; the command to take stones from the river in 4:5 is accomplished in 4:8. This pattern overwhelms the reader with a sense of obedience to divine commands and fulfillment of divine promises, and it provides guidance not available in a plot line.

Joshua 3:1—5:1 also has a discernible chronological movement, despite the overlapping subjects, temporal digressions, and narrative asides. Joshua 3 and 4 make up two basic segments of the narrative. Joshua 3 narrates Israel receiving instructions to cross the Jordan and then crossing over. Joshua 4 presents the orders for, and finally the creation of, a memorial of the event, albeit with some digression into the nature of the crossing itself (4:10–13).

Much attention has been given to the fact that chapter 4 contains three separate descriptions of memorial stones. Two of these descriptions concern the same set of stones. This is potentially confusing but in keeping with the overlapping and repetitive features of the narrative. I will suggest that these segments of the story have a logical arrangement that fits the overall purpose of the story.

46

In Joshua 4:1–7, Joshua, at the Lord's command (vv. 1–3), selects one representative from each of the twelve tribes to take a stone from the middle of the Jordan and transport it to "the place where you camp tonight" (v. 3). Verses 6–7 contain instructions on how the memory of these stones will be perpetuated. An explanatory "ceremony," prompted by a child's question, passes on the memory of the event to future generations (see Exod. 12:26–27; 13:14–15; Deut. 6:20–21). Verse 7 mentions explicitly that the stones were memorial to the fact that the waters of the Jordan "were cut off" in front of the ark. Verse 8 notes that the people carried out Joshua's instructions.

Joshua 4:9 reports that Joshua configured a set of stones in the middle of the Jordan as the priests carrying the ark stood there with the waters cut off upstream. This verse is written as an aside or a parenthetical comment (reflected in many modern translations) that seems to describe an action Joshua took while the twelve tribal representatives carried stones to the west bank of the river. The Greek translators recognized the potential for misunderstanding, with stones being carried across the river to the place of encampment and also stones being placed in the riverbed. Therefore, they added the word "other" before "stones" to make clear that there were indeed two memorials. A careful reading of the Hebrew (upon which our translations are based), however, shows this also to be clear in the original reading of the text. Indeed, the absence of a definite article ("the") before the word "stones" indicates that the Hebrew authors thought of these objects as a second set of stones, as the Greek version makes more explicit. This second memorial was probably intended as a marker to honor the priests who stood in the midst of the Jordan (Butler, *Joshua*, p. 49).

Joshua 4:19–24 refers to the same set of stones as 4:1–8, and verses 21–24 have virtually the same question and answer that appear in verses 6–7. This double description of the memorial stones has raised questions about the sources of the two sections and why both are included. Several striking differences between the two accounts indicate that they were composed by different hands. It is often proposed that Joshua 4:19–24 derives from a tradition based at Gilgal that did not include an experience with the ark (but see pp. 49–50, "The Hand of the LORD Is Mighty"). Nevertheless, in the present context these differences need not be interpreted as contradictions. The location at Gilgal in verses 19–24 does not conflict overtly with the previous account, since the location is not named earlier. There is also a logic to the presence of the two sections and their order in the narrative. The first set of instructions indicates that the stones are to serve as a memorial "to the Israelites" (4:7). The second instructions broaden the meaning of the event by recalling God's mighty deeds not only at the Jordan but also at the Red Sea. The intended impact of the event is also enlarged. Verse 24 indicates that the crossing is to make Israel "fear the Lord," but it also occurred that "all the peoples of the earth may know that the hand of the LORD is mighty" (4:24). This concluding statement of purpose is followed immediately by a report that the desired effect of God's act on the nations was achieved (5:1). The hearts of the Canaanites melted precisely because they heard of the Lord's powerful action in drying up the Jordan.

What the Story Teaches

To appreciate further the instructional character of Joshua 3:1—5:1 and what the story teaches, it may be helpful to imagine the account being composed by a committee made up of representatives from all Israelite traditions. The story's presentation of the ark of the covenant may be evidence that, in fact, such a process took place. The portrait of the ark and its impact seems to include something from virtually every Old Testament voice. The ark is known by the familiar label "ark of the covenant" (3:6, 8, 14; 4:9), which is the favorite language of the Deuteronomic tradition; it is also called "ark of the testimony" (4:16), a title that derives from Priestly circles. The effect of the ark upon the waters of Jordan is similar to the portrayal in stories that understand the object as the invisible throne of God that scatters Israel's enemies (Num. 10:35–36) and accounts of the ark striking people dead with its supernatural energy (1 Sam. 6:19). The recognition of Levitical priests as bearers of the ark and the order for the people to remain at a distance from it (3:3–4) resemble the Chronicler's view that the Levites had exclusive responsibility for carrying the sacred chest (1 Chron. 15:2). Most significant is the fact that some of the traditions that give rise to these descriptions and portraits of the ark disagree as to the significance of the object. This point has been classically expressed as follows: some circles saw the ark as representative of the presence of God (2 Sam. 6:2), while the Deuteronomic tradition downplayed its importance and spoke of it as a container for the Ten Commandments (Deut. 10:1–5). However overly simplistic this description of Israelite traditions might be, it helps clarify that the committee's assignment *was not* to delineate clearly the nature of the ark. Moreover, their task was not to explicate exactly the process by which Israel crossed the Jordan and set up memorial stones. That, as we have already observed, is somewhat uncertain. Indeed, what the story teaches is not so much about Israel or about this particular event at all but about the nature of Israel's God. Three claims about the Lord express the primary lessons of Joshua 3:1—5:1: the Lord is "the living God" (3:10); he is "Lord of all the earth" (3:11, 13); and "the hand of the LORD is mighty" (4:24). The fact that

48

the story intends to press these claims as lessons to be learned is evident from the contexts in which the statements about or descriptions of God appear. In each case the text says directly that the Jordan crossing or its memory is for the purpose of making known these truths.

"The Living God"

The expression "living God" occurs only eight times in the Old Testament in the exact form that appears here. In Hebrew, the word "living" comes after the word God. Therefore, the phrase could be translated "God, the Living One" to show that these two words constitute an official title (Compare the Hebrew of this term, *El ḥay,* to *El qannaʾ,* "God, the Jealous One," in Exod. 20:5). "Living God" seems to describe the Lord as one who has power to act on behalf of Israel. The label appears, for example, in Isaiah 37:4 and 17 (and parallels in 2 Kgs. 19:4, 16), in which Hezekiah says that the living God was mocked by the Rabshekah of Assyria when he declared that the Lord would be unable to deliver Israel. Similarly, in Joshua 3:10 "living God" is linked to what God will do for Israel, namely, "drive out from before [them] the Canaanites, Hittites, Hivites, Perizzites, Girgashites, Amorites, and Jebusites." What is less certain in Joshua 3:1—5:1 is how the living God is known in the context of the Jordan crossing. Joshua 3:10 declares, "By this you shall know that among you is the living God." "By this" may refer simply to the ark's appearance in the Israelite camp, as in Judges 4:5–9, where the mere presence of the object makes the Philistines afraid of Israel. "This" may also anticipate the ark's effect on the waters of the Jordan (3:13). As we shall see below, however, the ark's presence and the ark's impact on the river cannot be separated. As the expression of the living God's power, the ark's appearance meant that something awesome would occur.

"The Hand of the LORD Is Mighty"

"The hand of the LORD is mighty" (4:24) seems, on the surface, to be a broad figurative statement. But on closer examination it has quite concrete implications. The term "hand," an anthropomorphic way of speaking of the Lord's power, is sometimes used to speak about the ark. In 1 Samuel 4:8, when the ark came into Israel's camp, the Philistines declared, "Woe to us! Who can deliver us from the power (Hebrew = hand) of these mighty gods?" Given this background of the phrase "hand of the LORD," therefore, Joshua 4:24 implies that "all the people of the earth may know" of the Lord's might by the procession of the ark. This association of the Lord's hand with the ark is important in Joshua

49

4:19–24, since many critics have seen this passage as coming from a tradition at Gilgal that did not include the ark. The ark was so important an expression of God's power that it was often assumed to be present even when it was not mentioned specifically. This is the case in Psalm 24:7–10, which speaks of "the King of glory" entering the city gates (Ps. 24:7, 9). The liturgy involving the opening ("lifting") of gates for God's entrance almost certainly reflects a procession of the ark. So too in Joshua 4:24 the Israelites fear God and the people of the earth know of God's might as a result of seeing the ark pass by.

The statement about God's might made in the Jordan crossing is enhanced by the comment in 3:15 that "the Jordan overflows all its banks throughout the time of harvest." More than a note concerning the difficulty of the crossing, this is a kind of political statement that has "the peoples of the earth" in view (4:24). This description of the Jordan overflowing its banks is patterned after Assyrian texts that describe an army crossing the flooded Euphrates en route to battle (Van Seters, "Joshua's Campaign of Canaan," p. 7). Hence, the reference to the Jordan overflowing aggrandizes Joshua's army so that it appears like Assyria's, as is the case other places in the book (Josh. 1:4; 15:45–47). The message was that Israel had its own source of divine power that ultimately could not be overtaken. In the context of Assyrian and later Babylonian domination, this reference to the Jordan overflowing represents a resilient and resolute faith that Israel's God will bring victory to a people so often subjugated by the powerful empires of the world.

"Lord of All the Earth"

"Lord of all the earth" (Josh. 3:11, 13) is a special case that poses difficult questions of meaning and raises potential theological problems. As to the meaning of the expression, it is unclear whether the last word in the title refers to the land of Canaan or to the entire habitable sphere. The Hebrew term ʾereṣ can mean either. If the former meaning is intended, the title mainly expresses God's control over Canaan that permits God to give the land to Israel. Of course, this notion is clearly part of the theological claims of the story, but the question is whether the title should be understood more broadly as a statement of God's universal sovereignty. "Lord of all the earth" is used in this more expanded way in Psalm 97:5, Micah 4:13, and Zechariah 4:14 and 6:5. These parallel texts all come from the period after Jerusalem's destruction, as does the final form of Joshua 3:1—5:1. For the exilic audience of this story, it would have been important to know that the God who had power to deliver Canaan to Israel also had sovereignty over the nation that now held Israel in exile.

The theological problem comes in verse 11. In Hebrew, "Lord of all the earth" is juxtaposed to "ark of the covenant," so that the second phrase seems to define the first. Although most modern translations blend the two phrases together (NRSV: "the ark of the covenant of the Lord of all the earth"), the Hebrew construction requires "ark of the covenant" and "Lord of all the earth" to be read as two separate phrases that stand in apposition. In other words, the text seems to equate the ark with God, apparently in direct opposition to a pillar of biblical thought, namely, the idea that God cannot be seen or represented in any concrete form (Deut. 4:15–20). Some scholars have proposed that the title "Lord of all the earth" was inserted in 3:11 by an editor who had in mind the appearance of the label in verse 13, where it properly qualifies the divine name. The more "orthodox" wording in verse 13 should be a guide theologically. "Lord of all the earth" is intended as a description not of the ark itself but of the God whose power is expressed by the ark. Nevertheless, this does not alleviate the problem completely. The dilemma also arises in 4:13, which mentions the people crossing over "before the LORD" (i.e., passing before the Lord and before the ark seem to be equated). But two observations are important in this regard: First, the ark was never thought to represent God in any Old Testament tradition, though some texts, like Joshua 4:13, come close to this idea; rather, in the grandest view of the ark, the object signified the presence of God's throne. The Lord was still invisible. God was not and could not be captured in an image or likeness cast by humans, and the ark was not an attempt to do so. Second, it is significant that later generations that lived without the ark could still believe God was with them, that "the hand of the LORD is mighty." That indicates that the character of God, who was once symbolized by this sacred object, endured, even though the ark did not. God's presence was mediated later by other means, primarily the written word. In other words, the story in Joshua 3:1—5:1, with its *memory* of the ark and the Jordan crossing, became a symbol of God's might. Even after the ark ceased to exist, Joshua 3:1—5:1 would continue to remind Israel that its God was "the living God" and "Lord of all the earth."

Connections to the Theology of Joshua

Israel's Unity

In addition to the main theological points about God's character just discussed, this story also contains important theological themes that appear elsewhere in the book. For example, it presses upon the reader an understanding of Israel as unified people under the leadership of

51

Joshua. We see this in the declaration that "the Reubenites, the Gadites, and the half-tribe of Manasseh crossed over armed before the Israelites, as Moses had ordered them" (4:12). Joshua's authors go to great lengths to show here, as elsewhere in the book (1:12–18; 13:8–12; 22), that the territorial divide between the eastern and western groups was overcome by political and religious unity. Numerous times the story refers to "all Israel" (3:1, 7, 17; 4:14). The people are spoken of holistically, all in obedience to Joshua and the Lord. It is also significant that Joshua 3:17 and 4:1 describe Israel with the Hebrew term *goy*, usually translated "nation." This term is associated closely with the term "people" (Hebrew *'am*), a word that also describes Israel numerous times in the book of Joshua. The exact difference between the two terms is not always clear, but the word *'am* seems to communicate primarily blood relationships, while *goy* refers to a political entity (1 Kgs. 18:10; Isa. 60:12; Ps. 135:10). The use of *goy* here signifies a change in Israel's status when crossing the Jordan. They ceased to be a wandering band and became a landed people who would have to be dealt with as a political entity.

This depiction of Israel's unity under Joshua is strikingly different from the picture in the book of Judges of virtually the same time period. Indeed, Judges shows an Israel in which local families and tribal groups had significant freedom to act apart from the rest of Israel or to abstain from participating in the activities of the larger group. For example, Judges 5:15b–17 notes that Reuben, Gilead (probably a reference to Gad), Dan, and Asher did not answer Deborah's call to join the other tribes in battle. Here we get a picture of a loosely configured tribal league in which the strongest loyalty existed at the local level, particularly within the "household of the father," where blood relations were certain. As the family relationships grew outward to extended family and tribe, and simultaneously as blood relations became less sure, loyalty also grew less strenuous. Only a king's central authority could rein in such a diverse group for the common good of the whole. The book of Judges sums up this period by saying, "In those days there was no king in Israel; all the people did what was right in their own eyes" (Judg. 21:25).

In light of these other texts, it seems that Joshua 3:1—5:1 "flattens out" the picture of Israel by implying that Joshua had absolute authority, with little indication that local patriarchs or elders affected the political process (note the few references to elders and tribal chiefs in texts like 8:33; 20:4; 22:14; 23:2; and 24:1; these leaders do not exercise independent power in any story). This section of the book of Joshua remembers the age of Joshua as a time when such centralized hegemony

52

existed even without a monarch. The most important questions, however, are "Why?" and "What does this mean theologically?" Part of the
answer may be found in the larger delineation of the figure of Joshua,
who is presented as a royal figure, patterned after Josiah. This type of
unity was the political reality of the authors' time, and the book of
Joshua is cast against that backdrop. Another possible reason for the
anachronistic portrait, however, is more important theologically: this
sense of unity is part of Israel's self-identity at the time of the writing of
Joshua, and therefore it becomes part of Israel's memory of its foundation. Similarly, Americans, diverse in ethnicity and experience, tend to
adopt and identify with a single view of national origins. Settlements at
Jamestown and Plymouth have come to embody values for the nation
as a whole that collapse the variegated experience of immigrants into
one. In a similar way, Israel's unity or dreams of unity are read back into
its origins, into a period of time when the reality was surely quite more
complex.

Joshua's Exaltation

Another theological connection to the rest of the book concerns the
exaltation of Joshua. This subject is addressed explicitly in the Lord's
promise to create acclaim for Joshua among the people (Josh. 3:7) and
in the subsequent note that the people in fact stood in awe of Joshua
after the Jordan crossing (Josh. 4:14). The promise of 3:7 ties Joshua
directly to Moses. Then the continuation of the Lord's address to
Joshua in verse 8 further emphasizes his authoritative position by the
emphatic instruction, "*You are the one* who shall command the priests
who bear the ark of the covenant." The association of Joshua with Moses
as God's chosen leader continues themes expressed overtly in Joshua
1:5b and 17a and communicated implicitly in Joshua's sending of spies
in chapter 2. Hence, the Lord's address to Joshua in 3:7 and the confirmation of Joshua's exaltation in 4:14 are of a piece with the divine attitude toward Joshua thus far in the book.

Joshua 3:1–17 appears in the revised lectionary paired with
Matthew 23:1–12, a text that explores what makes a person worthy of
God's exaltation. The Gospel text states emphatically that those who
humble themselves and who do not presume to occupy Moses' seat will
be favored by God. Conversely, those who exalt themselves will be
humbled. In Joshua 3:1–17 the reason for God's exaltation of Joshua is
not spelled out. It is possible to see Joshua as one fit for exaltation, however, because he does not vaunt himself over his creator but instead
obediently waits for God's prompting. In the larger context of the book,
Joshua is a model of torah obedience; he shows dependence on God

53

by constantly meditating on the law and being perfectly obedient to the commands that came through Moses. The church fathers praised Joshua precisely for not exalting himself, even though he performed great signs, especially causing the sun to stand still over Gibeon (Josh. 10:12–13). This praiseworthy characteristic of Joshua is indeed Jesus' criterion for exaltation (see *The Ante-Nicene Fathers*, vol. 7, Apostolic Teaching and Constitutions, book 8, sec. 1).

Chapters 3 and 4 also portray Joshua as a prophetic figure. They do so in part through the impact of Joshua's instructions to the priests and the people. Two points are important in this regard. First, the account depicts Joshua, like Moses, receiving direct instructions from God and then proclaiming them to the people. Joshua's authors probably intend Joshua to be perceived as "a prophet like Moses," whom Deuteronomy 18:15–22 predicts God will raise up after Moses' death. Although the text never labels Joshua a prophet, his introductory words in 3:9b, "Draw near and hear the words of the LORD your God," are similar to the opening words of many prophetic oracles (Isa. 1:10; Jer. 2:4; Hos. 4:1; Amos 3:1; 4:1). The plural "words" is the only slight difference between Joshua's speech and the prefatory words of other prophets. Therefore, it is not surprising that the Greek, Aramaic, and Latin versions all record a singular term, "word." This change aligns Joshua's speech more closely with other prophetic discourse.

Second, the content of Joshua's speeches at the Jordan (3:9b–13; 4:5b–7) suggests that Joshua has authority not only to deliver the divine word but also to interpret and apply it. Indeed, Joshua does not merely repeat God's words verbatim; rather, he puts them in his own words and explains the significance of God's command with instruction on how the decree should be appropriated in the life of the people (see Polzin, *Moses and the Deuteronomist*, pp. 82–84).

The Role of Common Memory

Joshua 3:1—5:1 illustrates the importance of liturgy and ritual, which provide an interpretive memory of salvation events. James Gustafson has said that the church is shaped by a "common memory." This memory includes "knowledge about the past," but membership in the faith also requires "personal identification with the meaning of the past events" (*Treasure in Earthen Vessels*, pp. 71–72). Or, as Allen Verhey puts it, "Without remembering, there is no identity. In amnesia one loses one's identity. And without common remembering, there is no community" ("The Holy Bible and Sanctified Sexuality," p. 35). Joshua

3:1—5:1 demonstrates the importance of such a shared, meaningful memory. Indeed, it interprets the Jordan crossing for a later generation and inculcates a proper understanding of the event; it urges the audience to internalize its significance, to be moved by the story through a consciously created memory. Like Joshua 3:1—5:1, the church's formal remembrance of Jesus' suffering, death, and resurrection has historical roots, but the events are not so much reported as they are memorialized so that a theological lens is built into the telling of the story.

Joshua 3:1—5:1 also illustrates the need for people of faith to find tangible signs of God's presence. The Bible gives continual witness to God's being experienced in concrete ways, in people, places, and objects, which for Christians culminates in the experience of God in Christ (Terrien, *The Elusive Presence*, pp. 162–75). The story of the Jordan crossing shows how the ark served Israel in this way. The fact that the story endured after the ark was no longer present, however, also shows that no one sign of God's presence completely fills this need. As the New Testament makes clear, even the experience of God in the person of Jesus would give way to Jesus' memory, mediated by the Holy Spirit and passed on through the story.

Joshua 5:2–12
The Disgrace of Egypt Is Rolled Away

Transitions from one age to the next and from one generation to another are gradual. The interests and values of successive groups overlap. In light of that common fact, Joshua 5:2–12 makes a startling claim: not a single member of the wilderness generation entered the land! This definitive break was anticipated, of course, by stories of faithlessness in the wilderness (Num. 14:30; Deut. 1:35). But now Joshua 5:2–12 shows that wilderness epoch came to a clear and decisive end. Following the account of Israel crossing the Jordan, this segment of the book functions much like a curtain fall in the theatre: it tells the reader that the Israelites who were forbidden to enter Canaan have exited the stage, and now a new generation has entered to possess the land. Joshua 5:2–12 works in tandem with the book's opening emphasis on the death of Moses to show that the wilderness period is officially complete (Josh. 1:1–2). It does so through two vignettes: first, Joshua circumcises those Israelites born in the wilderness, making clear that all those who left

Egypt with Moses and were circumcised by him are dead (5:2–9); then Joshua leads the newly circumcised Israelites in the first Passover in Canaan (5:10); that celebration triggers an end to the manna that sustained Israel in the wilderness (5:11–12; Exod. 16:15).

Circumcision was a prerequisite for the Abrahamic people to gather before God (Gen. 17). For that reason Joshua circumcised the Israelites as preparation for the first Passover in Canaan, just as Moses circumcised those in Egypt before the very first celebration of this festival (Exod. 12:43–49). In Joshua 5:2–9, however, circumcision is also a sign that the torch had been passed from those Israelites who were circumcised by Moses before the exodus to their children born in the wilderness. A hint of this generational divide is carried in the Lord's command to Joshua to circumcise the Israelites "a second time" (Josh. 5:2). This reference does not suggest that God commanded Joshua to circumcise men who had already undergone the rite. Rather, as verse 5 states, all males coming out of Egypt had been circumcised, but Israel had not observed it with the children born in the wilderness.

Some scholars think the original story of this second circumcision is found in the Greek version (the Septuagint), and that the Hebrew (upon which our translations are based) contains later changes to the account. Whether or not this theory is correct, a comparison of the Hebrew and Greek texts helps to highlight the sharp division between the two generations that our English translations record. The Greek version states that Joshua circumcised those born in the wilderness *as well as* some who were not circumcised in Egypt. The Hebrew text, with a pronounced emphasis on the break between these two groups, says that those who came out of Egypt were all circumcised but they "perished, not having listened to the voice of the LORD" (v. 6a). Therefore, "it was their children, whom he raised up in their place, that Joshua circumcised" (v. 7). Hence, the Hebrew text gives evidence of a theology clearly distinguishing the generations of Moses and Joshua.

The theological divide between generations is enhanced by the location of Joshua's circumcision at Gilgal. The temporal reference "at that time" (5:2) sets the circumcision in that period immediately after Israel crossed the Jordan, and 5:9 states explicitly that Gilgal was the site of the event. The name Gilgal derives from a Hebrew verb meaning "to roll"; hence, the place is identified as that location where the "disgrace of Egypt" was "rolled away" when Joshua circumcised the Israelites born on the way to Canaan (5:9).

56

The exact meaning of the expression "the disgrace of Egypt" is uncertain, but it clearly refers to shame borne by the Israelites in the wilderness. In the early development of the story these words may have referred to the fact that some Israelites came out of Egypt uncircumcised (as reported in the Greek version) and that this problem was corrected at Gilgal. In the present book of Joshua, however, the phrase has a slightly different meaning; it refers either to the humiliation of Egyptian bondage, humiliation that did not end until Israel settled in its own land (see the similar expression in 1 Sam. 17:26), or to the wilderness generation's lack of faith. These two interpretations are complementary. In Joshua's theological schema the wilderness generation never completely shook off the stigma of Egyptian bondage, because it was not willing to accept the freedom of land possession. The wilderness wanderers carried a disgrace that they could not remove, since they had a "life sentence" that disallowed their realization of the promise of Canaan.

This claim that Joshua's group removed the disgrace of the previous generation has interesting theological implications. The text infers that the sins of parents can be expiated later by the right actions of their children. Specifically, the disgrace of the wilderness generation, which is beyond their power to remove, is erased in the act of circumcising their offspring. Jeremiah and Ezekiel both address the issue of how one generation's *sinfulness* impacts the next. They refute the notion that the sins of parents cause suffering for their children (Jer. 31:29–30; Ezek. 18:1–4). But Joshua 5:9 goes one step further to declare that God sometimes atones for the parents' sins through the faith of their descendants. The writer of Hebrews declares that the church is in continuity with its heroes of faith and is responsible for bringing their work to fruition (Heb. 11:39–40). Joshua 5:9 is similar in its emphasis on the connection between generations, but it insists that by their faith those who possessed Canaan covered for their ancestors who died in the wilderness because of their lack of faith.

The significance of the circumcision of Joshua's generation is particularly pronounced when read against the exilic backdrop of the final form of the book. Since circumcision was practiced regularly in Egypt and among most other West Semitic people, the rite would not seem unique while Israel lived in Canaan. But in Babylon, where circumcision was not common, it became a significant mark of devotion to God. Joshua's exilic audience likely read the account of Joshua circumcising Israel in a new land in light of their presence in Babylon. Understanding this setting in exile may prompt questions about what marks contemporary people of faith as distinctive. How does the church stand apart from the surrounding culture and give witness to its faith? That was undoubtedly a pressing question for the exiles in Babylon, and Joshua 5:9 may have provided one answer.

Joshua 5:13—6:27
The Lord Conquers Jericho

"By faith the walls of Jericho fell after they had been encircled for seven days" (Heb. 11:30). With this characterization of Joshua 5:13—6:27, the writer of Hebrews captures the essence of the Jericho story. Jericho's defeat was a great sign of Israel's trust in God. Indeed, the story is crafted so that it cannot be reduced to an account of human triumph over great odds. Joshua 6 reports no military strategy, no troop movements with a recognizable purpose, no calculated attack on the city walls; human achievement in the battle is all but denied. By portraying the victory in this way, Joshua 5:13—6:27 illustrates the book's opening claim that Canaan was God's gift to Israel (Josh. 1:3) and that military prowess would not win the land.

Although the basic lines of this well-known story are clear, this section of the book is complex and confusing in some of its details. For example, there are conflicting reports as to who is blowing trumpets in the procession around Jericho. In 6:8 and 13a it is the priests who go in front of the ark, but in 6:9 and 13b it is the rear guard. Although modern translations smooth over the problem by rendering, "trumpets *were blowing*" in verses 9 and 13b, the Masoretic Text implies that members of the rear guard were doing the blowing. One possible explanation for this problem is that the story began as a more traditional battle report but was gradually altered to emphasize the celebratory aspect of the event as it was later reenacted in worship (see Soggin, *Joshua*, pp. 86–87). Whether or not this is true, the present narrative features God, represented by the ark, as the primary actor and Israel as the recipient of divine aid. Whatever confusion may remain in the text, it is not great enough to prevent that point from coming through loud and clear.

But the theme of God's initiative in capturing Jericho also has a rough edge. The account emphasizes that the contents of Jericho must be returned as an offering to the Lord, as the first fruits of conquest. Hence, Israel's strict observance of regulations regarding items "devoted for destruction" (Hebrew *herem*) is proper response to God's defeat of the city. This poses difficult questions about how Joshua is to be appropriated to the life of faith: How may the church claim the story as Scripture when it sanctions the killing of innocent people? Is there some way to read the story that makes it more palatable? The following discussion will explore the purpose and meaning of the ban in the story. The first task, however, is to show how the story is structured and how

58

it works as a story, with particular attention to the way some formal elements of the account thwart the reader's expectations.

The Commander of the Army of the Lord (5:13–15)

The theme of God's defeat of Jericho arises for the first time in Joshua 5:13–15, a brief and somewhat cryptic story about Joshua's encounter with a mysterious heavenly figure who identifies himself as "the commander of the army of the LORD." This account was likely placed before Joshua 6:1–27 to introduce the story of Jericho's fall with a word of assurance that the Lord would win the battle for Israel. That purpose is confirmed by a strikingly similar account in the annals of Assyrian king Assurbanipal. He reports that the goddess Ishtar, with drawn sword like a warrior, appeared to his advisor to promise support in an approaching battle. Although the stories are not identical, and the biblical conquest account is vastly different theologically from Assurbanipal's documents, still the Assyrian record provides the best suggestion for why Joshua 5:13–15 appears where it does (see Van Seters, "Joshua's Campaign of Canaan"). To discern what this story attempts to say as an introduction, it is necessary to examine some of the problems in the text that have often hindered scholars in seeing its purposeful place in the book.

The difficulties of discerning the role 5:13–15 plays in the book stem in part from evidence that it did not originally introduce 6:1–27 and that vestiges of an earlier purpose remain. For example, the opening reference to Joshua's location "by Jericho" (Josh. 5:13) might better be rendered "in Jericho." Some have thus concluded that the story once narrated an event that occurred after the Israelite forces entered the city. Others have suggested that the mention of a "holy place" indicates that 5:13–15 originally was set in a sanctuary, probably Gilgal (see Miller, *The Divine Warrior in Early Israel*, pp. 128–31).

The literary form or genre of 5:13–15 exacerbates the problem of its place and function in the book. The story begins much like a commissioning report, similar to the tale of Gideon's call in Judges 6:11–24, for example, and the story of Moses' commissioning in Exodus 3—4. Such stories typically include four parts: (1) a human meets God or an angel; (2) the human responds in fear or worship; (3) the deity or angel appoints the human to a specific task; (4) God or a heavenly representative gives a sign of assurance that the task will be successful. Joshua 5:13–15 includes the first two elements of this story type, thus creating the expectation that Joshua is about to receive instructions concerning

59

his role in the ensuing battle. The expectation is intensified when Joshua asks, "What do you command your servant, my lord?" (v. 14). Moreover, verse 15 alludes to Moses' appointment (Exod. 3:5) and thereby heightens further the anticipation of Joshua's specific call. But, with the reader's attention pricked for Joshua to receive an assignment, the narrative ends with a barefoot Joshua—like Moses at the burning bush (Exod. 3:1–6)—who has been given nothing to do.

These features of Joshua 5:13–15 indicate that it was adapted to its current place in the conquest story. But what exactly does it say as introduction? We should notice, first, that despite the possible association with a sanctuary in the story's past, it is about the ensuing conflict between Israel and the residents of Jericho. The heavenly commander's drawn sword, Joshua's question as to which side he is on, and his self-identification as leader of a heavenly army all make that clear (see Num. 22:23; 1 Chr. 21:16). Then it seems important to notice how 5:13–15 thwarts expectations about Joshua's commissioning (the question of genre). Some scholars have speculated that the story was abbreviated and that the task given Joshua was removed when the story was added to 6:1–27, since 6:2 already included God's instructions to Joshua. This may be the way the story developed, but in its present shape and position the shortened commissioning form also communicates a distinctive theological message. The abbreviated call story helps make known the fact that Joshua's primary task is to be steadfast in faith. In this regard, the reference to Joshua standing in a holy place (5:15a) may be an interpretive key. The designation "holy" uses the same word that describes the precious metal objects that are placed in the Lord's treasury (6:19). In the context of the final form of the story, Jericho is holy in that it is devoted to divine use and will be captured only through divine effort. In light of that fact, it makes sense that Joshua's commission would be to rely on the divine warrior. His primary "task" in the conquest is the one he received at the opening of the book, namely, to trust that God would secure the land for Israel (Josh. 1:1–9).

The commander of the Lord's army and his role in the Jericho battle pose problems for many modern readers who resist the notion of divine involvement in human affairs. Indeed, modernity insists that humankind is the moving force in history, which implies that God is removed from the process. Joshua's authors, on the other hand, assumed the opposite. They believed that God was an effective power in history; as part of history (not lord over it), humanity could do little to change or control it but was subject to its divinely initiated movements (see Schroeder, *History, Justice, and the Agency of God*, pp. 37–39; and pp. 90–93, commentary on Josh. 10:1–14). Nevertheless, modern readers may take comfort in the fact that Joshua does not recognize the Lord's commander! In fact, Joshua's initial question to him might be termed "modern" in that it acknowledges only two forces in the approaching battle: "Are you one of us, or one of our adversaries?" (5:13). The commander's reply, "Neither" (literally, "No"), indicates that Joshua's question was wrong. A third force, a divine force that the commander represented, would determine the battle's outcome. When Joshua was jarred into that reality, he quickly did obeisance (5:14). The Greek translators omitted the reference to Joshua's worship of the commander, undoubtedly because they thought it was blasphemous to bow to an angel. Similarly, some Christian interpreters have reasoned that the heavenly figure was Christ, because "a created angel dared not receive" Joshua's worship (Wesley, *Commentary on the Bible*, p. 154). The first audience of the story, however, would not have differentiated sharply between the commander and God who sent him, as indicated by similar Old Testament stories (Gen. 16:7–14; Judg. 6:11–24; 13:2–23). Joshua's reaction to the commander of the Lord's army is an essential part of the story. It indicates that Joshua was faithful in response to his "call"; he put himself in the hands of the divine warrior, confessing implicitly that his own military prowess would not be as important as his sincere prostration before God.

The Lord's Defeat of Jericho (6:1–27)

The story of Jericho's fall in Joshua 6, like its introduction in 5:13–15, works in part by presenting surprises in what it reports and how it reports it. The modern reader, however, may need a bridge to the world of ancient Near Eastern warfare in order to understand just how the account thwarts expectations.

It is important first to understand the nature of the city the Lord delivers to Joshua in chapter 6. The archaeological evidence indicates that Jericho may have been a rather insignificant agricultural village in the late Bronze Age (1550–1200 B.C.; see Mazar, *Archaeology of the Land of the Bible*, p. 331). But Joshua 6 assumes Jericho in its glory days. Jericho boasted a significant population with a defensive wall around the settlement perhaps as early as 10,000 B.C., making it the world's oldest walled city. Visitors to the site today can view a thirty-foot-high fortified tower that dates to the Neolithic period (6800 B.C.), an illustration of the defensive capability that existed when the city was at its peak.

The primary objective in campaigns against fortresses like Jericho was to penetrate the city's defensive walls and gates. Therefore, the key point of the "battle" in Joshua 6 is the felling of Jericho's walls, which provided access to the city and left the residents of the city virtually helpless before the attackers. Ancient invaders penetrated such a citadel by one of three methods: (1) sometimes they entered the settlement by ruse; the parade example of this technique is the Greek story of the Trojan horse, but it is also employed in Joshua 8; (2) at other times the army assaulted the city directly by breaking through, going over or under weak places in the city's defenses (e.g., city gates, indefensible points in the wall); (3) a third option was to lay siege to the fortress, cutting off supply lines until residents were forced to surrender. When Joshua 6:1 notes, "Jericho was shut up inside and out," it indicates that the city's residents had prepared themselves for a direct attack on its defensive walls (which could lead to siege if the assault failed).

Military strategy also included a theological component. Typically, a military leader sought a prophetic oracle to determine whether going to battle was prudent (1 Kgs. 22:5–18). The Lord's response then was formulated in stereotypical language such as, "I will give _____ into your hand" (1 Kgs. 20:28).

Some ancient battle reports have God devising strategy for the army. We see this in Joshua 8 when the Lord tells Joshua how many troops are needed for the battle at Ai and then commands Joshua to lay an ambush. The Ai story is a good example to set in contrast to Joshua 6. The report about Israel's defeat of Ai features a recognizable strategy that is used as a result of God's directive. In Joshua 6 there is no military assault. The account of the attack on Jericho does follow a typical pattern in many ways. God's word to Joshua is like that in other battle reports, "See, I have handed Jericho over to you" (v. 2). Moreover, Joshua repeats the message to the warriors in v. 16b: "Shout! For the LORD has given you the city." But despite these similarities to other battle reports, the story does not indicate that Joshua sought the Lord's advice about going to war, much less do so as part of preparation for an attack. On the contrary, the story begins with God giving Joshua an unsolicited word about his success. Hence, the reader is not led to see Joshua planning an attack strategy; instead, Joshua is prompted and led by God at every turn. The promise to hand Jericho over to "you" does use a second person singular pronoun. Joshua alone is addressed as though he is a great military commander who goes forth to conquer. Nevertheless, he does nothing to defeat the city, and his command to shout, a sign of engagement in battle, comes after God has already felled Jericho's walls.

Most importantly, Israel acts contrary to any known military procedure in its attack on Jericho. Israel's actions do *resemble* known military tactics. For example, when Israel encircles the city, the act is *similar* to the procedure of setting up posts at strategic points around the settlement in preparation for an attack on the city's walls and gates. But the text clearly says that the circuit around Jericho is not for that purpose. Indeed, the Lord does not order Joshua to position soldiers around the city wall. Instead, "all the warriors" encircle the city and then return to their starting point (vv. 3, 7, 14). The circuit around the city is a ritual procession, closer to a liturgy than any recognizable military action.

It is probably not accidental that the Israelites encircled Jericho on seven days, the same period as the Passover festival. Hence, the taking of Jericho not only follows Passover in the book but also unfolds like Passover, as a festival celebration. The procession around the city includes trumpet-blowing priests in the lead. The Hebrew word for the priests' horn is *shofar*, a ram's horn, which was used as a signal for warfare (Job 39:25) but also played a prominent role in worship (2 Chr. 15:14). The procession around Jericho has the ark as the central element, like the ritual crossing of the Jordan in 3:1—5:1. Of course, the seven-day pattern does not necessarily suggest a festival. Certain key events, such as the glory of the Lord covering Mount Sinai, lasted seven days (Exod. 24:15–16). The seven-day span generally represents completeness and signals the successful realization of a task or event (1 Kgs. 20:29). Nevertheless, the intended impression seems to be that the first two weeks of Israel's life in Canaan were occupied with religious celebrations. The first was Passover (5:10–12), and the second was the ritual-like battle at Jericho.

Jericho as Firstfruits

When the Israelites had circled the walls of Jericho seven times on the seventh day of their encampment against it, Joshua gave instructions concerning how the city should be captured. The treatment of Jericho is shaped almost completely by the notion that this first city of the conquest was to stand in perpetual ruins as a monument to the great victory God won for Israel there. As some expositors have observed, Jericho was the "firstfruits" of the land (Wesley, *Commentary on the Bible*, p. 155; Calvin, *Joshua*, p. 95). Joshua's first command concerning the taking of Jericho was that "[t]he city and all that is in it shall be devoted to the LORD for destruction" (6:17a). Here the ban is comprehensive; nothing is to be left alive, and the city itself is to be burned. The complete destruction of the city indicates that Jericho is to be like a whole burnt offering, completely destroyed as a gift to God. This probably also explains the curse Joshua issues in 6:26. Although the

63

meaning of the curse is disputed, and it is possible to explain the prohibition against rebuilding Jericho by means of other theories, the easiest explanation is that Jericho was to remain a constant ruin because the city as a whole was "devoted to destruction."

The concept of the ban is confusing to Western readers both because it is foreign culturally and because the concept in the Old Testament itself is complex. A fuller knowledge of the idea is necessary to appreciate its appearance in Joshua 6. As a feature of warfare, the ban is known among other ancient Near Eastern people, as evinced by the mention of the practice in the Mesha Inscription or Moabite Stone (Pritchard, *Ancient Near Eastern Texts*, pp. 320–21). Some scholars have speculated that the ban was implemented for practical reasons; destruction of whole populations may have been an attempt to prevent disease or to deny an opposing army any resources. Regardless of these possible motivations for the practice, the records about the ban from the ancient world, including the Old Testament and the Mesha Inscription, understand the ban as a purely religious issue. Deuteronomy presents it primarily as a matter of justice (Deut. 7:2, 26; 20:16–20). Moses commands Israel to "utterly destroy" the inhabitants of the land (Deut. 7:2; 20:17) and to "show them no mercy" (Deut. 7:2), not letting "anything that breathes remain alive" (Deut. 20:16) precisely because these people may "teach you to do all the abhorrent things that they do for their gods" (Deut. 20:18). In other words, the Canaanites are to be destroyed because they are iniquitous, and their worship of other gods may spread to Israel if it is not eradicated (Deut. 9:4–5).

The notion of the ban in Joshua 6, however, cannot be explained fully by the Deuteronomic law. As we have observed, the story seems to conceive the ban as a sacrifice to God, as though God required the contents of Jericho as an offering. This difference between Joshua and Deuteronomy is indicated in part by their different uses of the Hebrew root *ḥrm*, from which come the verbal expression "utterly destroy" (or "devote to destruction") and the nominal phrase "devoted thing." Deuteronomy primarily uses verbal forms ("utterly destroy") since it commands Israel mainly *to do* something, namely, to obliterate the residents of Canaan in order to rid the land of their idolatry. In contrast, Joshua 6:17 includes a nominal form, which emphasizes the fact that Jericho is *to be* something: "the city shall be a devoted thing; all that is in it belongs to the Lord" (NRSV: "The city and all that is in it shall be devoted to the LORD for destruction"). Joshua's instruction in 6:18 further clarifies this view of the ban as sacrifice. He warns Israel to "keep away from the things devoted to destruction," lest the Israelite camp become "an object for destruction, bringing trouble upon it." The notion that one could become an object for destruction by possessing a "devoted thing" stems from the idea that the items to be banned were the Lord's portion. As such these items were holy and should not be handled carelessly. This point is illustrated by Joshua's subsequent command to place the precious metal objects into the treasury of the Lord because these items are "sacred to the LORD" (6:19). These objects became holy when dedicated to God by means of a vow (which Josh. 6:17 probably implies). In any case, the point is that, as holy objects, any human possession of them caused humans to be contaminated. The reference here anticipates the story of Achan in chapter 7. His unauthorized contact with the "devoted things" causes a plaguelike disaster to begin spreading to all in his tent.

In its use of the noun form of the Hebrew root, *ḥrm*, Joshua 6:18 is similar to Leviticus 27:28, which speaks of the possibility of people, animals, and land being designated as *ḥerem*, things devoted to destruction. This regulation is sometimes referred to as the "peace *ḥerem*" because it seems to apply to ordinary time, not to a time of war. Nevertheless, the law in Leviticus may be understood broadly as background to Joshua 6 in two details: (1) those items designated as "under the ban" were to be sacrificed; (2) humans under the ban could not be redeemed; that is, money or other gifts to the temple or sanctuary could not be given in their place (Num. 3:40–51). The fact that the Israelite invaders were not permitted to possess anything in the city and that rebuilding the city was prohibited (6:26) indicates that Jericho was to be treated as a kind of offering to acknowledge that God won the battle.

The Redemption of Rahab

The particular concept of the ban in Joshua 6 may seem grotesque compared with that in Deuteronomy. Indeed, Deuteronomy is generally thought to show awareness that the subject is offensive and therefore rationalizes the ban, as many Christian interpreters have done, by couching it in terms of justice. The notion of the ban as a sacrifice, which dominates Joshua 6, seems more primitive. Yet the ban's barbaric character is mitigated by the way it is portrayed in this story. Namely, this chapter's presentation of Rahab as a prominent exception to the ban may signal an attempt to soften it. Indeed, in the segment dealing with the ban, each command concerning the devoted things is followed immediately by a reference to Rahab's salvation (vv. 17b, 22–23, 25). There is a pattern of (1) commands to destroy the devoted things followed by (2) instructions to save Rahab. It is possible to see in this pattern an example of a glass half empty. *Only* Rahab is saved from

65

destruction. There are clues in the text, however, that suggest we should read in the opposite direction. Rahab's salvation is particularly significant in light of the known regulations regarding the ban. Neither Deuteronomy nor the Leviticus text cited above makes room for exceptions. In fact, Leviticus 27 concludes with an emphatic denial of the possibility of redeeming any person who has been offered on oath as a devoted thing: "No human beings who have been devoted to destruction can be ransomed; they shall be put to death" (Lev. 27:29). Yet the directive is blatantly broken in Rahab's case. As one of the "devoted things" of Jericho (v. 17a), she is destined for destruction, but she is redeemed instead. Rahab continues to be treated as a "devoted thing." She is placed outside the camp (v. 23) because, as the Lord's possession, she could not be kept as a slave, taken as a wife, or "owned" in any sense by an Israelite. Moreover, as a "devoted thing" Rahab must remain at a distance so the Israelites do not become infected with the sacred nature that required her destruction. But she is not slain. Hence the story does not focus attention on the multitude that is slaughtered. Instead, it draws attention to the fact that the only Jericho resident who is named, whom the reader can relate to and sympathize with, is spared annihilation.

There is some evidence that the early church read the Rahab story as a sign of God's grace. As early as A.D. 333 pilgrims visited a site in Jericho identified as Rahab's house. The primary attraction was that this structure survived Joshua's attack on Jericho. Almost certainly, what visitors saw was a house that had been built for the sake of the "tourists," as many such places were established during the Byzantine period. Nevertheless, it is significant that the early church identified Rahab's house as a monument to God's salvation. It signified that God preserved some outside the elect of Israel and that in fact such "exceptions" really characterized the rule of God's grace for humankind (Noort, *Das Buch Josua*, pp. 145–46).

Sacrificial Imagery and Language

The Rahab story anticipates the salvation story in the New Testament in its use of sacrificial imagery and language. The early church shared with ancient Judaism the idea that God required sacrifice. Hence, some early Christian preaching declared that Christ's death satisfied God's desire for ritual offering (1 Cor. 15:3). An important part of this sacrificial model of salvation is the idea of redemption. That is, some who are destined for ritual slaughter can be preserved if a substitute is offered. This idea was particularly applied to the work of Jesus in that he was sacrificed so that all others might be redeemed.

The notion continues as an undercurrent of the church's theology, as expressed in the third verse of the hymn "Go to Dark Gethsemane":

> Calvary's mournful mountain climb;
> There, adoring at his feet,
> Mark the miracle of time,
> God's own sacrifice complete.

Rahab's story anticipates this theology. Although many modern people cannot get past the Old Testament assumption that God might desire and even require human sacrifice, to focus on this ancient idea is to miss the point. The Rahab story, and later the Christian story, works with and sublimates the notion that God desires sacrifice by declaring that God sacrificed his own son (see Levenson, *The Death and Resurrection of the Beloved Son*). Without this sacrifical idea as background, much of the biblical notion of Jesus' death makes no sense. Rahab's redemption is, in a sense, the firstfruits of the full redemption that will be accomplished in the work of Jesus.

Appropriating the Word of God

The ban in Joshua 6 is also linked to an understanding of the word of God and how it is appropriated. The problem turns on the fact that certain regulations concerning the ban that were authoritative for Joshua (particularly Deut. 20:10–20; but perhaps also Lev. 27:28–29) are abrogated in the story. Rahab and her family members are prominent exceptions to Joshua's command to destroy all the residents of Jericho. Their salvation can be explained only as a sign of grace, albeit grace that Rahab sought and obtained through her cunning. The preservation of the harlot cannot be fitted into any of the loopholes in known instructions about *ḥerem*. The Israelites essentially treated Rahab as one who accepted terms of peace (Deut. 20:10–18), but she dwelt in a city that was not to have such terms offered. Yet Joshua is affirmed at the end of the account (6:27), and later evaluations declare he was faithful to all Moses commanded (10:40; 11:12, 15).

How is this possible? If obedience means applying the written word like a set of assembly instructions, then Joshua cannot be conceived as obedient. But this is clearly not how the book is evaluating Joshua's application of the commands of Moses and the Lord. We have already seen that Joshua is free to relay divine instructions in his own words and with supplemental commentary and explanation (see pp. 43–55, commentary on Josh. 3:1—5:1). In other words, the word of God is understood as dynamic. It has theological intentions that must be

67

treated with utmost seriousness, but it does not and cannot account for every circumstance that may arise. The people of faith must appropriate the word afresh in each new situation, open to the Spirit's leadership into new truth based on the word.

In Reformed theology, part of the dynamic of Scripture is the notion that a text may be interpreted by other texts. This is often applied to the conquest by saying that Joshua should be read alongside biblical visions of peace and nonviolence. The redemption of Rahab illustrates the point that some texts contain this tension within themselves. Rahab's salvation is evidence that Joshua's authors themselves were concerned about the implications of the ban and so presented the ban as a backdrop for what was most important, namely, a presentation of God's salvation and rescue from destruction.

Joshua 7
The Lord's Anger Burns against Israel

If Joshua 5:13—6:27 is an illustration of Israel's faith, accepting God's gift of Jericho and offering its contents back as the firstfruits of the conquest, Joshua 7 depicts the opposite. This section tells how a certain Achan took some of the booty from Jericho and brought the Lord's wrath upon Israel. He stole what was rightfully God's, an act arising out of an arrogant sense of autonomy and a blatant disregard for divine authority.

This story of Achan's sin and execution is, at points, troubling and confusing. It raises questions about crime and punishment that are particularly difficult: Who is responsible for taking the devoted things from Jericho? Is it Achan alone, Achan and his family, or all Israel? If only Achan is guilty, as he implies in his confession, "I am the one who sinned against the LORD God of Israel" (Josh. 7:20), why is his family killed with him? As we attempt to answer such questions, we will continue to wrestle with the notion of the ban: In what ways does the ban act as an instrument of justice? How does the ban relate to ideas of holiness, sacrifice, and keeping covenant? In the final analysis these questions will not be resolved completely. But some level of uncertainty on the other side of discovery illustrates the untidiness of rebellion against God and the human attempt to eradicate it. These problems are at the heart of Joshua 7.

Literary Structure and Logic of the Story

The story of Achan's sin and punishment is set within the larger account of Israel's attack on Ai. Joshua 7:1 informs the reader that Achan took some of the devoted things from Jericho and that the Lord's anger burned against Israel because of this unfaithful act. References to divine anger frame the account of Achan (vv. 1 and 26). The first mention of God's wrath lets the reader know in advance why Israel is turned back from the initial attempt to defeat Ai. Then Joshua 7:2–5 summarily reports how the Israelites scouted the city, attacked it with a small force of about three thousand men, and were driven back and defeated by the city's defenders. This brief account of Israel's defeat is like Judges 7:1–23, in which Gideon led a reduced force to victory. While the size of Gideon's small army signified Israel's reliance on the Lord, however, Joshua's reduced number of soldiers showed Israel's overconfidence and ignorance of the Lord's anger directed towards them. In Joshua 7:2–5 the spies, not God (as in the Gideon story), develop the attack strategy. Furthermore, Israel attacks Ai without any word from the Lord that the battle will be successful, in contrast to Israel's action at Jericho (Josh. 6:2). Hence, Achan's sin of taking goods from Jericho is also an illustration of the larger Israelite problem with autonomy. At Ai the Israelites assume they can go it alone, so they develop their own military strategy apart from the Lord. As a representative member of the group, Achan acts as though he is entitled to some of the spoils of battle, as though Israel's military acumen gained the victory.

Joshua intercedes for Israel, but he is not privy to the cause of the defeat. His petition reveals a strategy similar to the one Moses used in the golden calf episode (Exod. 32:11–14). Like Moses, Joshua argues that God's reputation will be damaged if Israel falls short of possessing the land (7:9). This manner of addressing the Lord may seem manipulative; it is certainly not a type of prayer familiar to most modern Christians. It makes sense, however, and is perfectly acceptable in light of the contractual nature of ancient Israelite society and the assumption that God, too, acted in contractual ways. Like any human member of society, the Lord would naturally be concerned if perceived as one who did not keep covenant obligations. So Joshua seizes this point as a way to argue with God and to gain God's attention for Israel.

In 7:10–15 the Lord answers Joshua with a speech that corrects his perception. The divine address to Joshua has two primary parts. In 7:10–12 the Lord changes Joshua's understanding of why the defeat

69

occurred. This segment begins with God's order to Joshua to alter his stance, from prostrate, in fearful worship, to upright and ready for hearing (v. 10). The Hebrew here includes two imperatives, "arise" and "go," that work in complementary fashion and are appropriately translated together as a verb pair that communicates one message: "Stand up!" After correcting Joshua's posture, God declares Israel's sin and vulnerability. In Joshua 7:11–12 the Lord reveals that Israel became "devoted for destruction" by its possession of items under the ban and that the Israelite army would suffer defeat until the devoted things were destroyed. The second half of the Lord's speech to Joshua (vv. 13–15) begins like the first, with the imperative that literally means "Arise!" Since the word is followed by a purpose clause, it is rendered aptly, "Proceed" (to sanctify the people; v. 13aα). The sanctification of the Israelite camp is to be done by purging it of the "devoted things" (7:13aβ–15). Joshua 7:16–26 includes the report of Joshua carrying out the Lord's instructions. Verses 16–21 focus on the identification and charge of Achan as the one guilty of stealing the devoted things. Verses 22–26 conclude the Achan story with the record of his death. The act of burning recognizes that Achan has become like an object for sacrifice. His body is then covered with stones to form a memorial cairn that remained as a reminder of the troublesome event (vv. 25–26; Achor, close to the sound of the name Achan, means "trouble" and appears in verbal form in Joshua's question in v. 25). The Achan story ends with a second reference to God's anger, this time a note that the divine wrath was assuaged by Achan's death (v. 26).

The Nature of Sin and Punishment

The modern emphasis on the individual has led to a popular understanding of sin as a single act committed by one person. The individual has freedom to choose good or evil, so the thinking goes and therefore is responsible for whatever misdeeds he or she commits. Modern theologians often point out, of course, that sin is also corporate; the individual, though free to "refuse the evil and choose the good" (Isa. 7:15), is caught in a web of evil that spawns and perpetuates rebellion against God. As Hendrikus Berkhof puts it, sin is interpersonal in that every deceitful act is due in part to the influence of other people. It is also suprapersonal, that is, evil is systemic in the human community, and the individual cannot escape it (*Christian Faith*, p. 213). The Achan story illustrates well this sense of human interconnectedness in sin, so much so that the categories of individual and community, though clearly present in the story, are blurred at numerous points. Indeed, in Joshua 7 the

70

questions of who is guilty, who should be punished, and why are sometimes difficult to answer.

Joshua 7:1 introduces the Achan story with three points that show the interplay between individual and corporate responsibility. Verse 1 begins by saying that "*the Israelites* broke faith in regard to the devoted things." Then, specifically how they sinned is explained by pointing to the action of Achan, who "took some of the devoted things." Having identified Achan as the perpetrator of evil, the verse concludes, "[T]he anger of the LORD burned against *the Israelites*." These statements make clear that, although only one person acted contrary to covenantal regulations, the whole community was held in contempt because of it. Furthermore, when God reveals to Joshua why the battle at Ai was lost, he declares simply, "*Israel* has sinned" (7:11aα), and in subsequent statements the Lord emphasizes that the whole nation is guilty:

> "*[T]hey* have transgressed my covenant that I imposed on *them*. *They* have taken some of the devoted things; *they* have stolen, *they* have acted deceitfully; and *they* have put them among their own belongings. Therefore *the Israelites* are unable to stand before their enemies." (7:11aβ–12aα)

The entire nation became a thing devoted to destruction, as Joshua warned in 6:18. As we shall see below, part of the dynamic of this story is the sacredness of the devoted things Achan took. They were imbued with a sort of virus that could infect the whole camp. This story is like others in the Old Testament in which cultic impurity brings punishment upon the community, not just on the perpetrator of the act (Lev. 10:1–7; Num. 16). For ancient Israel, however, cultic purity was bound up with covenant faithfulness. Therefore, the story indicates that Israel as a whole was not simply in danger of being infected by the one who mishandled items for worship; rather, the whole community was also guilty of violating the torah. Indeed, the text says that Israel, not just Achan, "broke faith" (7:1), "sinned" (7:11), "transgressed" the covenant (7:11), took devoted things (7:11), and "put them among their own belongings" (7:11).

Israel's corporate guilt gives an interesting cast to the proceedings in 7:16–26. Even though Israel as a whole sinned, the nation would be spared if the one directly responsible for the breach of covenant was removed. Therefore, Joshua identifies Achan as the guilty party by bringing forward kinship groups, beginning with the largest group, the tribe, and proceeding to the smallest, the individual household (Josh. 7:14–15 and 16–18). This progression of kinship units gives structure and increasing intensity to the search for the one who took the devoted things from Jericho. Probably by casting lots, Joshua first identifies the tribe of Judah (7:16). A tribe was a large group that included a host of families. Tribes were bound together in theory by blood relationships, but such relations were hard to prove. As the units got smaller, however, so did the certainty of bloodlines and the intensity of commitment of one member to another. The most cohesive social unit is referred to as the household of the father. This group consisted of a patriarch along with his sons and their families. Achan was a grandson of Zabdi, the head of a household, and the son of Carmi (7:1; note Achan's strong affiliation with his maternal grandfather in 7:24). This societal structure too reveals a sense of group identity and corporate sin. Achan brought shame on the household of Zabdi and the whole tribe of Judah in his unfaithful action.

In the end Achan is singled out for punishment. But why? Given the strong statement of corporate sin at the beginning of chapter 7 and in the speech of the Lord to Joshua (7:11–15), it is hard to imagine the nation's culpability being removed. Some scholars have suggested rightly that Achan was a scapegoat; indeed, in a society with such a pronounced view of corporate guilt, someone or some subgroup must bear the brunt of divine judgment so the whole community is not destroyed. God's wrath was assuaged through the death of Achan and the rest of the nation was allowed to live on. And yet at the point of Achan's execution it becomes clear that for ancient Israel an individual could not stand completely alone in sin or punishment. Though Achan was singled out for execution, his entire family was killed with him. Most modern readers are troubled by this part of the story and struggle to understand it. It is tempting to explain the death of Achan's family by the belief that the ban was "contagious" and that his close relatives and livestock were exposed to the ban by virtue of their presence in a tent that contained the devoted things. Although the authors of the story surely assumed such an understanding of the ban, it is not necessary to explain the destruction of Achan's household. Indeed, Israel's communal identity, particularly the identity of members of a household to each other, was so strong that the individual could not be conceived as completely autonomous. As Leo Perdue says, "In the household, individual will and needs merged into the collective will and needs of the larger whole" (*Families in Ancient Israel*, p. 237). This "collective will" extended to sin and punishment. The sins of one family member affected every other member, especially in the case of the head of the household, who embodied the values and actions of the entire group. This becomes clear when we recognize that Achan's sin is a negative parallel to Rahab's right action. When Joshua 7:15 says that the guilty

72

one, "together with all that he has," shall be destroyed, it uses a phrase identical to the one that describes Rahab's family in 6:25. In both cases the Hebrew reads woodenly, "and all that (or who) belongs to her/him." Hence, Rahab's act of harboring the spies preserves her family, while Achan's faithless deed dooms his. Her righteousness was extended to her household, just as Achan's disobedience caused his entire family to be implicated in his crime.

This interplay between individual and communal guilt has profound implications for contemporary views of crime and punishment. It suggests that when justice is meted out to individuals, correction is endured by societal representatives who embody, to some degree, the ills of the larger community. So, for example, Joshua 7 might encourage us to see those who populate prisons and those who die in state-sponsored executions as scapegoats for all society's ills. Such an appropriation of the Achan story can have the positive effect of correcting a view of sin that is often too individualistic. But on the other hand, the fact that Achan's family perished with him, though presumably innocent of stealing "devoted things," may seem to go too far in the other direction. The individualism of modernity rightly questions the fairness of "punishing children for the iniquity of parents" (Exod. 20:5). Nevertheless, although the kind of community and family orientation in Joshua 7 may shortchange the individual at times, it corrects modernity's imperious claims of the individual's autonomy. Moreover, the same cultural impulses that encouraged the death of Achan's family also gave rise to a theology that declared, "There will be no one in need among you" (Deut. 15:4). Such theological convictions that arise from a sense of corporate well-being were, according to Acts 4:32–37, integral to the theology of the early church.

Holiness, Covenant, and the Ban

As we have already observed, this story poses difficult questions about the ban and shows that its implementation is an important part of Israel's covenant obligation. Joshua 6 introduced the idea of the ban; some basic points bear recalling (see also the Introduction). Joshua 7, like Joshua 6:18, speaks of the ban primarily as a state of being, not an action. Put another way, in the stories of Jericho and its aftermath, the ban is not so much something to be practiced as it is the condition of being set apart for divine use. The only "action" expected of Israel was its complete abstinence from any person or object designated as a "devoted thing." This indicates that Israel's view of the ban was closely associated with its understanding of ritual purity. Just as

Israelites became unclean by touching a ritually impure item or person, so also they became "devoted for destruction" by mishandling a "devoted thing."

Because the ban in Joshua 7 is part of the covenant relationship with God, the failure of Israel to observe it properly is discussed in covenant language. Vocabulary from the Decalogue is prominent. The Lord characterizes Achan's sin as stealing (7:11), using the same words that appear in the eighth commandment, "You shall not steal" (Exod. 20:15; Deut. 5:19). When Achan confesses that he "coveted" the devoted things, he expresses his sin with the language of the final commandment, "You shall not covet your neighbor's house" (Exod. 20:17; Deut. 5:21). Regardless of whether or not these terms in Joshua 7 are intentional allusions to the Ten Commandments, the meaning of the charge against Israel is similar. The second half of the Decalogue intends to shape the behavior of fellow Israelites so that each respects the other's possessions. Orderly human community was possible only if the Israelites abided by such limits of property. Similarly Israel's relationship with God could be right only if Israel acknowledged that certain things and people belonged to God. "Stealing" what was rightfully God's threw off the relational balance between Israel and the Lord.

The covenantal aspect of Israel taking the devoted things is important for understanding the expression of God's anger in Joshua 7:1. The word rendered "anger" may also mean "nose" (Song 7:4), reflecting the ancient Near Eastern idea that this body part was the seat of emotions. Hence the statement that God's anger "burned" creates an anthropomorphic image of the Lord's nostrils flaring, or of the Lord snorting like an enraged beast. This expression most often describes God's anger at Israel when Israel breaks covenant (Josh. 23:16; Judg. 2:20) or pursues other gods (Deut. 31:16–17). Therefore, it may be helpful for modern readers to imagine God expressing anger here like a lover who steams over the infidelity of the partner. It is this type of anger within relationship that Joshua 7 has in mind (see pp. 128–30, discussion of God's jealousy in chap. 24).

The "Devoted Things" and the Christian Life

The relationship of the ban to ritual purity in particular provides important guidance for reflection on this concept, in that Joshua 7 precludes an easy equation of the ban practiced at Jericho with genocidal practices in recent history. The issue in Joshua is not so much ethnic purity as it is purity in worship and devotion to God (for fuller discussion see Niditch, *War in the Hebrew Bible*, pp. 56–61).

This perspective on the ban helps clarify what the ban does *not* say to contemporary society. It is more difficult to determine any positive message Joshua 7 might have for the church. One possible way to gain such insight is to follow early exegetes who assumed this text had a symbolic meaning. By this approach, the story may be read as a set of symbols that represent other realities. For example, Origen said that the "devoted things" in Joshua 6:18 represent the affairs of the present world. Therefore, he proposed that the text be applied to the church in imperatives like, "Do not mix the things of the world with the things of God" and "do not allow the affairs of the present world to enter the sanctuary of the church" (*Homélies sur Josué*, p. 205). Origen further linked this story's allegorical message to the plain sense of Paul's words in Romans 12:2, "Do not be conformed to this world."

Origen's interpretation illustrates the helpful principles that difficult texts should be read in light of other texts and that texts with no apparent theological value may be illuminated by more transparent texts. Nevertheless, historically minded modern readers have typically rejected this type of interpretation on grounds that it does not reflect the plain sense of the text in its original context. Indeed, Joshua 7 addresses a particular person who stole items that had peculiar significance. To be sure, the historical trappings of the Achan story should give guidance in interpretation. Origen was insightful, however, in his identification of the basic problem Achan's story poses. Achan was lured by the prospect of material gain, and he was willing to risk his soul to obtain this world's pleasures. The story *is* about the choice between the values of two worlds, the choice between holiness in covenant with God and prosperity obtained by secular greed. The preacher or teacher who deals with this text must admit the distance at which the contemporary audience stands from the story of Achan and the strangeness of the ban to the church today. Nevertheless, Joshua 7 has potential to speak powerfully to a dilemma all people of faith face, namely, how to be devoted to God while turning from the temptation to profit at the expense of faith. Achan is a primary illustration of one who could not come to terms with this choice (compare Acts 5:1–11).

At the heart of Achan's struggle is a problem with human autonomy or, rather, a false sense of human autonomy. The idea that some human actions are actually stealing from God is based on the belief that humans are ultimately dependent on the Lord for their existence and that a certain portion of life or possessions should be given to God as confession of that fact. Denying that creator-creature relationship is the root of sin. Or, as Søren Kierkegaard so aptly wrote, the sense of human adequacy is the primary barrier to genuine faith. Whether expressed as confidence

75

in science, moral progress, or military might, the human feeling of self-reliance distances a person from his or her creator (*Philosophical Fragments*, p. 24). Achan was someone who acted as though human power had won a battle and thus denied his dependence on God.

Joshua 8:1–29
The Lord Turns from His Anger

As we have already noted, Joshua 7 is framed by references to the Lord's anger, which burned against Israel because of Achan's sin (7:1) and then subsided when Achan and his family were executed (7:26). Joshua 8:1–29 is a continuation of the Achan story in that it tells how Israel attacked Ai a second time after the Lord turned from his rage over Achan's breach of covenant. Although Joshua 7 and 8:1–29 go together, however, the story of Israel's defeat of Ai raises its own particular questions that deserve independent treatment.

The Portrait of Ai

Joshua 8:1–29 portrays Ai as a major city, with a significant walled fortification, much like Jericho. Indeed, the strategy of luring Ai's defenders out of the city's ramparts makes sense only if the walls and defense towers are formidable, since the ultimate goal of the attack is to broach these barriers. Archaeological evidence about Ai in the thirteenth century B.C., the likely time of Israel's possession of the land, however, gives a very different picture of this town. Namely, the site identified as biblical Ai was indeed an impressive stronghold from about 3100 B.C. until 2400 B.C., but it was destroyed at that time and left uninhabited until about 1200 B.C., when the site began to be used as an *unwalled* village (Callaway, "Ai," p. 127).

Scholars interpret this evidence in a variety of ways. Some conclude that Joshua's authors (or the tradition on which they rely) confused Ai with Bethel, the important worship center located only two miles to the west (see Josh. 7:2), which *was* destroyed in the late Bronze Age (1550–1200 B.C.). Yet the story in final form knows of Bethel's proximity and even states that soldiers from Bethel came to defend Ai (8:17; though the reference to Bethel's assistance is ambiguous; it could be evidence that the story was originally about Bethel; the matter is complicated further by the fact that the Greek version does not include the reference to Bethel helping in the battle; and see the discussion in the next section, "Israel's Strategy at Ai"). Others understand Joshua 8:1–29 as an etiology that explains the ruins at Ai, attributing the destruction to Joshua's invasion (though, according to this theory, the city lay in ruins when the Israelites arrived). This theory is supported by the fact that the only name given for the city, Ai, means "the ruin" (see 8:28). If the city was razed by the Israelites, one might expect the story to reflect a *name change*, with the identification of the site as "the ruin" beginning with that battle (see Callaway, "Ai," for this and other possible interpretations). It is important to notice that Joshua 8:1–29 presents the battle at Ai almost exactly like a battle at Gibeah recorded in Judges 20. In both stories a city is defeated by ruse after a reprehensible act devastated the community. Therefore, it is possible that the authors of Joshua 8:1–28 employed a stock story form to explain how Ai came to embody its name (Auld, *Joshua, Judges, and Ruth*, pp. 55–56).

Although some of the archaeological evidence about Ai leaves questions concerning the historicity of Joshua 8:1–29, the theological portrait of the city is much clearer and is consistent with other portions of the conquest story. Ai is presented as a powerful city, comparable to Gibeon (Josh. 10:2) and Jericho (Josh. 8:2). Specifically, Joshua 8 is framed by references to the king of Ai (vv. 1 and 29), thus emphasizing the role of Ai's king and painting the settlement as a location of royal hegemony. As we shall see in Joshua 10—11, the "conquest" story largely depicts a revolt against the powerful kings of Canaan along with the trappings of their power.

Israel's Strategy at Ai

The story of Israel's defeat of Ai works in part by means of a striking contrast between the invaders, led by Joshua, and the residents of the town, headed by their king. After its sound defeat in its first attempt to capture Ai (Josh. 7:2–5), Israel shows complete deference to the Lord in its second attempt. Whereas in the first encounter with Ai Joshua sent spies and planned and carried out an unsuccessful assault, all apparently without seeking God's guidance, Joshua 8:1–2 reports that the Lord initiated new plans to take the city and then Israel complied fully with his instructions. The attack worked by means of a ruse. Israel stationed a portion of the soldiers behind the city. The remainder of the forces was located north of Ai, in sight of the town's residents. Ai's defenders failed because of a tactical mistake due to overconfidence; namely, all the city's warriors pursued the Israelites north of the city, leaving the citadel open to ambush. This picture of Ai's overconfidence is particularly

77

pronounced if the reference to Bethel in verse 17 is read as "house of God," which is, of course, what "Bethel" literally means. Ancient Near Eastern citadels often included a temple that was fortified and served as an inner fortress; such buildings were the last retreat when the town was invaded. It is possible that Bethel, house of God, in verse 17 refers to such a structure. If so, it is an emphatic statement that every soldier, down to the last man, came out of Ai to pursue Joshua's army.

Joshua, for his part, shows complete reliance on the Lord in the battle with Ai. Although he gives instructions for the battle, his words are in accord with what the Lord ordered (v. 8). Moreover, Joshua's leadership in the battle itself amounts to his holding up a sword "until he had utterly destroyed all the inhabitants of Ai" (v. 26). The word that designates the sword Joshua held is an unusual term; it refers to a sickle-shaped weapon, somewhat obsolete by the biblical period, but still used as a symbol of hegemony, as evinced by ancient Near Eastern artwork. Joshua's holding such an implement has two implications: (1) he appears in this story like Moses, who held up his hands throughout the battle with Amalek (Exod. 17:11; Sir. 46:2); (2) by holding this symbol of power, Joshua points to the might of God, who wins the battle for Israel. This latter point is reinforced when Israel places Ai's residents under the ban, showing in the city's conflagration that the city is God's property (although the livestock and spoil are taken as booty). In sum, Joshua 8:1–29 shows Israel being properly dependent on God, in contrast to their failure to do so in chapter 7. Furthermore, the account emphasizes the victory of God's people over a city that is characterized by royal power, power that will be confronted again and treated in more detail in chapters 10 and 11.

Joshua 8:30–35
Just as Moses Commanded

Joshua 8:30–35 may seem quite humdrum following the fascinating stories of the capture of Jericho, the apostasy and execution of Achan, and the defeat of Ai. Indeed, this text's detailed talk of the type of stones used for an altar, the exact positions of groups in relation to Levitical priests, and Joshua's writing the Mosaic law on stone pillars seems to pale in comparison to the rich narrative material that precedes it. This brief section, however, is just as integral to the book's theology and has the potential of speaking meaningfully to the contemporary church. One scholar goes so far as to say Joshua 8:30–35 is "the summit of the book of Joshua" because it shows so clearly obedience to the Mosaic law (Gelin, *Josue*, p. 57). Specifically, this section depicts Joshua fulfilling Moses' instructions in Deuteronomy 27 (see also the briefer reference in Deut. 11:29–30). In that chapter Moses commands the Israelites, upon entry into the promised land, to gather on Mount Ebal and Mount Gerizim for a celebration of covenant reaffirmation. They are to build an altar of unhewn stones on which they offer up burnt offerings as sacrifices to God and "good will" offerings that provide a communion meal for those participating in the ceremony. Then they are to inscribe the Mosaic torah on a set of plaster-covered stones and set up the stones as a permanent statement of Israel's fidelity to the constitution Moses delivered from God. Joshua 8:30–35 reports that Joshua carried out these instructions almost exactly as described in Deuteronomy 27 (examples of slight differences: Joshua specifies the makeup of the assembly in 8:35; Josh. 8:32 is unclear as to whether the law is copied on the altar stones or another set of stones).

The Place of Joshua 8:30–35 in the Book

As is often the case with theologically important texts, there are issues in the interpretation of Joshua 8:30–35 that must be resolved if the text's implications are to be understood fully. The location of this passage in the book is one such problem. The Greek version (the Septuagint) places Joshua 8:30–35 after 9:2, and a fragmentary copy of Joshua found among the Dead Sea Scrolls (4Qjosh[a]) locates the story before the circumcision in 5:2–9. What is more, these alternative locations of Joshua 8:30–35 might seem more logical than the Masoretic Text's order. What follows Joshua 8:30–35 in MT seems awkward, at least at first glance. Joshua 9:1–2 says that the kings in the land planned war against Israel when they "heard of this." The present arrangement of material suggests that "this" refers to the ceremony in 8:30–35, but the Canaanite offensive would seem more likely in reaction to Israel's military activity at Jericho and Ai. Hence, we are pressed to discern the logic of the location of Joshua 8:30–35 in the Masoretic Text and in modern translations.

A careful reading of Joshua 8:30–35 shows that the placement is in fact meaningful and that attempts to "correct" it in the ancient versions may miss its significance. Indeed, the arrangement in the Masoretic Text makes sense when we consider the Canaanite reaction to the covenant renewal (recorded in 9:1–2) in relation to the content of the renewal ceremony (recorded in Deut. 27—28). As already noted,

79

the present location of 8:30–35 suggests the Canaanite kings respond violently to Israel's recommitment to the Mosaic torah. The ceremony, which involved building an altar, could have been perceived as a land claim, a claim that would have inflamed those who controlled the territory. But most importantly, Joshua 8:34 implies that Joshua read all the blessings and curses in Deuteronomy 27 and 28 during the gathering. That being the case, the following promises to Israel would have certainly offended the kings of Canaan:

> [T]he LORD your God will set you high above all the nations of the earth. (Deut. 28:1)

> The LORD will cause your enemies who rise against you to be defeated before you. (Deut. 28:7)

> All the peoples of the earth shall see that you are called by the name of the LORD, and they shall be afraid of you. (Deut. 28:10)

When we consider these statements to Israel, the placement of 8:30–35 before 9:1–2 is quite logical. The Canaanite rulers recognize that Israel is declaring international superiority for itself, and universal sovereignty for its God. The recalcitrant kings of the land declare war, being unwilling to submit to the Lord's authority. Like the nations described in Psalm 2:1–2, the Canaanite kings "conspire" and "plot in vain," setting themselves "against the Lord" and Joshua, his appointed ruler. Thus, in its present location Joshua 8:30–35 testifies with many other Old Testament texts to the Lord's cosmic hegemony on the one hand and to the nations' failure to submit to his authority on the other hand (see the commentary on Josh. 8:1–29 and 10–12).

The Location of the Ceremony

Many modern scholars have also noticed a problem with the geographical location of the covenant renewal ceremony in Joshua 8:30–35. The event takes place in the pass between two mountains, Ebal and Gerizim, with groups of Israelites standing on each side. Between the two mountains, at the very site of the ceremony described in Joshua 8:30–35, stood the city of Shechem, one of the most important settlements in the region. Shechem played a very important role in the history of Israel's patriarchs. This is the first place Abraham is said to visit as he passed through Canaan (Gen. 12:6); Jacob had a close connection to the city; this town was the scene of the rape of Dinah (Gen. 34). Joshua 24:1 explicitly mentions Shechem as the location of Joshua's final address to the Israelites, but scholars have often noted that this location is surprising in 8:30–35 because it represents a move some 20 miles north of the victory at Ai with no record of other battles that opened this northern territory. But what is most puzzling is that Joshua 8:30–35 never names Shechem as the site of the covenant renewal! Moreover, the Deuteronomy texts from which Joshua 8:30–35 draws also omit the name of the place, evidence perhaps that the name of this city is purposefully left out of the discussion. The problem is complicated by the fact that Deuteronomy 27:2 orders the ceremony to take place "on the day that you cross over the Jordan," suggesting that the location of the event must be Gilgal (see 3:1—4:24), even though it says the altar is to be set up on Mount Ebal. Deuteronomy 11:30 may be an attempt to smooth over the difficulty with its curious statement that Mount Ebal and Mount Gerizim are "opposite Gilgal." Some have proposed that these texts reflect the merging of two traditions, one that placed the event at Gilgal and another that knew the ceremony at Shechem. Another creative solution to the problem is that Mount Ebal and Mount Gerizim were represented by mounds of stones at Gilgal by the Jordan (we must realize also that the Old Testament knows more than one place named Gilgal). Whether this second theory is correct historically, it is most helpful in understanding the presentation of the event in Joshua and the orders for the ceremony in Deuteronomy. Indeed, it is clear that the present form of Joshua 8:30–35 paints a picture of Shechem in the reader's mind, but at the same time the larger context gives the impression that Gilgal is the location of the ceremony.

The occurrence of the event at or near Gilgal would be logical, since this Israelite base camp was a chief holy site where a monument had already been set up (4:19–24). Moreover, it is the place Israel arrived "on the day" they crossed the Jordan, and it is near Jericho and Ai, which are defeated just before the covenant renewal. Further, the following chapter says the Gibeonites find Joshua at Gilgal when they seek to make a covenant with Israel (9:6). But why describe the place in a way that draws images of Shechem? The answer is that ancient Shechem was associated with covenant-making, just as Athens was affiliated with philosophy, or Geneva is identified with diplomacy today. The city's chief deity was called the "lord of the covenant" (this is the meaning of the name Baal-berith in Judg. 9:4; also Judg. 9:46 mentions a temple of El-berith, "God of the covenant"). It is hard to imagine any ancient author in the region who was not aware of this specific role the city played in covenant making. Hence, the description of the place for the ceremony in 8:30 and 33 portrays it as an ideal spot for reaffirming the agreement between God and Israel that had been established through Moses (see pp. 118–30, commentary on Josh. 24).

81

There is also some uncertainty concerning the altar that is constructed and on which sacrifices are made as part of the ceremony described in Joshua 8:30–35. As Graeme Auld points out, it is odd that the altar is located on Mount Ebal since it is to the left as one stands at Shechem and looks at the two mountains and the left hand is considered sinister in biblical thought (*Joshua, Judges, and Ruth*, p. 61). Indeed, the altar is located on the same hilltop from which the covenantal curses are pronounced (Deut. 27:13). When the Samaritans later identified this place as their most sacred site, they recorded Mount Gerizim, to the right, as the place Moses ordered the altar to be built!

Significance of Covenant Renewal for the Church

This short segment of the book has important implications for the whole, particularly given the placement of the passage in the book. Since the book began with a command to Joshua to "act in accordance with all the law that my servant Moses commanded you" (1:7), Joshua 8:30–35 functions like a midterm report. It assures the reader that Joshua is faithfully keeping Moses' commands and acting appropriately as Moses' successor. As the text accomplishes these purposes, the passage also directs the reader's attention away from warfare and conquest. It makes clear that Joshua's most important role is to lead Israel in covenant loyalty. The book of Joshua ends with a similar portrait of Joshua (chap. 24). Thus, Joshua 8:30–35 marks a midpoint of his successful completion of a life and calling to meditate on the law of Moses continually (Josh. 1:8), as well as a literary midpoint between the command of Moses in Deuteronomy 27—28 and the final covenant renewal in Joshua 24.

Yet the picture of Joshua obeying the instructions of Moses raises the question for the modern reader, What portions of the Mosaic commands from Deuteronomy 27—28 are applicable today, and in what ways are those commands instructive for the contemporary community of faith? In what way does Joshua provide a model of torah obedience for the church? As we have already observed, there is great ambiguity about some details of how the ceremony in Joshua 8:30–35 is carried out, for example, the place the covenant renewal ceremony occurred. Shechem and Gilgal seem to have been conflated, making impossible a clear identification of either place as *the* proper location of the event. Also, the location of the altar, just as the place of the ceremony itself, is uncertain and should not be taken as having enduring significance for the church's interpretation.

82

What clearly stands out in Joshua 8:30–35 is Joshua's attention to and publication of the law of Moses before the Israelite congregation.

The text says he first "wrote on the stones a copy of the law of Moses" (8:32) in the presence of all Israel (8:33, 35) and then "read all the words of the law" to them (8:34). Hence, Joshua put forward the torah of Moses as the standard by which Israel should live, and he did so in the presence of the whole community. The preacher may find in this torah renewal at least two important implications for the church. First, the community of faith is called to submit to the Lord's authority and to shape itself according to God's vision of justice. This point is sharpened when we realize that the only previous reference to a "copy" of Moses' law is in the context of the king's subordination to the Mosaic legislation (Deut. 17:18). The community of faith is not to be an autocracy, in which one person exercises dominion. Nor is it to be a democracy, with all parties deciding together their common will. Rather, the covenant community is to be a theocracy, every person seeking *God's* intention and being shaped by a divine purpose. That purpose is described in the Mosaic torah, which was intended to act as a kind of constitution for ancient Israel (see pp. 27–29, commentary on Josh. 1, "The 'Book of the Law' and the Modern Reader"). Second, Joshua 8:30–35 carries an implicit message about the importance of public witness to God's grace and a public commitment to obedience. The text speaks to notions in some Christian circles that blessing can be obtained without righteousness and that victorious living can be had without sacrifice.

Joshua 9
Saved by Trickery

The Gibeonites are introduced for the first time in Joshua 9. They are identified as Hivites, a group that migrated to Canaan from Anatolia several centuries before the Israelite presence in the land. Therefore, they are quite distant from Israel in cultural and territorial identity. And yet they are remarkably similar to some key figures in Israelite tradition in the techniques they use to advance themselves! The Gibeonites are cut from the same mold as characters like Jacob, Joseph, and Tamar in that they are marginalized figures who improve themselves through manipulation. They are like Jacob particularly, since they use trickery in order to gain something they would otherwise be denied. Moreover, in the context of the conquest story the Gibeonites resemble Rahab, a successful and vindicated trickster (Josh. 2; 6:17b, 22–25). They and Rahab are preserved because of their wily action, even though they should be destroyed according to stipulations about the ban (Deut. 20:10–20; see the Introduction). Therefore, the reader is drawn into sympathy with them in part because their character type and story is so familiar. Ancient Israel probably had an affinity for such characters, even non-Israelite figures in their midst, because it conceived itself as a constant underdog that gained its place in the world through God's help, but also through cunning and deception.

Structure and Plot

Joshua 9:1–2 sets the stage for the Gibeonite story by reporting that the kings "beyond the Jordan" planned to go to war with Israel. The story then naturally divides into two sections. Verses 3–15 report the Gibeonite covenant, while verses 16–27 narrate the angry reaction of Israel when they learn they have been tricked. The first portion of the narrative is particularly interesting since it seems to tell the story from a Gibeonite point of view, as opposed to the second section, which gives the Israelite perspective. Indeed, verses 3–15 portray the Gibeonites as clever and intellectually superior to the Israelites. It is to their credit that they "acted with cunning" (v. 4). The Hebrew term rendered cunning sometimes has a negative connotation (Job 5:13; Ps. 83:3), but here it has the sense of prudence (as in Prov. 15:5 and 19:25). This appreciation for the Gibeonites' cleverness may seem strange to many modern Western readers, since it amounted to telling a bald-faced lie. For that reason, contemporary readers may need some help to comprehend the worldview that could see such trickery as laudable. It is helpful to understand the contractual nature of ancient Near Eastern society and how deceptive figures like the Gibeonites might function within such a context.

In ancient Israel a covenant or treaty was taken with utmost seriousness. It was made on oath before God, and its revocation carried dire consequences, since the oath usually included a self-curse that invited God's wrath if the agreement was broken. Therefore, the ancient reader of Joshua 9 would have likely focused immediately on the fact that a covenant was made and only secondarily on the Gibeonites' "unethical" means of obtaining it. Moreover, for a perpetual underdog like Israel, the Gibeonite attempt to make a covenant with Israel was a kind of contest, a test of wits in which the shrewdest group prevailed and was praised for it, regardless of what method they used. This does not mean that Joshua 9 or similar stories praise or encourage deception and lying. Nevertheless, this account is like the cycle of stories in Genesis 25—27 in which Jacob obtains what was rightfully Esau's. From the biblical author's perspective, Jacob is not so much deceptive (a fact that is obvious) as Esau is dull and undiscerning. Similarly, Joshua 9 portrays the Israelites as impulsive and slow of mind. They make a covenant without first seeking the Lord; and they are easily fooled by the Gibeonites' story of a long journey and moldy provisions (could the travelers not have obtained fresh bread on the journey?). Because the Israelites do not consider such questions, they are duped by the quick-minded Gibeonites, who, like Israelites in many other stories, are fighting for their survival. Although the story does not say it, the Gibeonites actually fit in with the Israelites quite well, given their tactics in this story.

When the Gibeonites approach Joshua's men, they do so with all the proper conventions of a vassal before a suzerain in an ancient Near Eastern treaty. They use standard diplomatic language when they say, "make a treaty with us" (v. 6; literally, "cut a covenant with us"). They politely introduce their purpose by saying to Joshua, "We are your servants" (v. 8). They bring provisions for a meal to seal the pact (v. 14). The Israelites are deceived by their charade, and they share the meal with the Gibeonites. Then, verse 15 says, Joshua "made peace with them," and the people swore an oath of faithfulness. As we have seen already, however, verse 14b reveals Israel's foolishness; ancient Near Eastern treaties were made in view of the gods, but Israel did not "ask direction from the LORD" before they made their oath. Nevertheless, although their treaty with the Gibeonites put them at odds with their covenant with the Lord, particularly the agreement not to make covenants with other nations (Deut. 7:2), they could not revoke the oath. Such a solemn vow was like an arrow that, after being fired from a bow, could not be retracted. According to the larger biblical story, the pact would pay long-term dividends to the Gibeonites. Second Samuel 21:1–14 reports that David took up the Gibeonites' cause when the Lord revealed to him that Saul was guilty of breaking the treaty. David avenged the Gibeonites by impaling seven of Saul's sons at the town of Gibeon.

The second portion of the story seems so different in perspective that many scholars have suggested it was composed separately and later joined to verses 3–15. According to this view, verses 16–27 explained the later slave status of foreigners during the reign of Solomon (1 Kgs. 9:15–22). This may be so, but the two parts of the story fit nicely together in present form, with verses 16–27 forming the natural sequel to verses 3–15. In verses 16–21 the Israelites discover the Gibeonite trick and travel to their cities to confront them. Because an oath had been sworn, the Israelites do not attack, but they do implicate the leaders for their hasty covenant making (v. 18). In verse 21a the leaders

85

insist that the Gibeonites remain alive. The verse then concludes (v. 21b) that the Gibeonites became "hewers of wood and drawers of water," with no comment on the reason for that role or whether it was positive (denoting a privileged status) or negative (referring to a punishment or reduced status). Verses 22–26 then reiterate these themes, but emphasize Joshua's leadership. Joshua's question in verse 22 and the subsequent curse in verse 23 imply a court proceeding. The curse placed upon the Gibeonites clarifies the statement in verse 21b as an imposition of lower status, but service in the temple hardly seems overly punitive, if Psalm 84:10's praise of such service is taken seriously!

The story clues the reader to the fact that the residents of Gibeon are like Rahab and should be classified with her. Unlike the other residents of the land, they acknowledge the power of Israel's God and prudently seek exemption from the ban. Indeed, the Gibeonites, who heard "what Joshua had done to Jericho and to Ai" (9:3) and then "acted with cunning" (9:4), are like Rahab, who upon hearing what God had done for Israel connived her way into an agreement with the Israelite spies. In contrast to the other Canaanites in 9:1–2; 10:1–5; and 11:1–5, the Gibeonites, like Rahab, acknowledge that Israel's success is due to the action of Israel's God, not simply to military prowess. The outline of the Gibeonites' speech in 9:9–10 is strikingly similar to that of Rahab's confession in 2:9–11. Like Rahab, they recognize that it was the Lord who was displacing the people of Canaan (2:9; 9:9); they "heard a report of him," not of Joshua's army, just as Rahab heard that "the LORD has given you the land" (2:9). Furthermore, a variant reading of verse 3 states that the Gibeonites heard what the Lord (not Joshua) did at Jericho and Ai. If this wording is original, it increases the sense that these people recognized God at work in Israel's presence. But regardless of that point, the Gibeonites' own speech indicates they heard of God's liberating action in Egypt (9:9) and of what he did to Sihon and Og east of the Jordan (2:10; 9:10), and responded in fearful submission.

Certain texts from Deuteronomy loom in the background of Joshua 9 and provide a frame of reference that gives meaning to the story. For example, the story makes subtle use of vocabulary and themes from Deuteronomy 29. The description of the Gibeonites' worn-out sandals and clothing (v. 5), which the Gibeonites themselves emphasize in verse 13, recalls Moses' speech in Deuteronomy 29:5, in which he declares that the Lord did not allow Israel's clothes and sandals to wear out. When Joshua discovers the Gibeonite deception, he pronounces a curse on them that reflects the status of sojourners described in Deuteronomy 29:11. More important for the theology of Joshua 9, the Gibeonite action assumes the Gibeonites know the regulations about the ban in Deuteronomy 7 and 20, and the story as a whole runs on a track created by these laws. Indeed, when in Joshua 9:24 the Gibeonites explain why they deceived the Israelites, they betray knowledge of Moses' command concerning the Canaanites that "you must utterly destroy them" and "make no covenant with them and show them no mercy" (Deut. 7:2). Their specific deception also assumes they know the distinction between the inhabitants of cities that the Israelites will inhabit in Canaan and those far away (Deut. 20:15). The Gibeonites create the impression that they are coming from a great distance by wearing worn-out clothes and sandals and carrying moldy provisions. Disguised as distant neighbors, they come to Gilgal and petition Joshua, "We have come from a far country; so now make a treaty with us" (9:6). They represent one of the groups in Canaan that decided to attack Joshua to avoid destruction (9:1). But unlike the other members of their group, these Hivites wisely decide on a different strategy to ensure their future in the land.

Escaping the Ban

Obviously, the point of Joshua 9 is that the Gibeonites, aware of Israel's mandate to destroy all occupants of the land, escape the ban by tricking Israel into a covenant. As we have already noted, this classifies the Gibeonites with Rahab, who acts similarly. The conception of the ban in Joshua 9, however, is somewhat different from that in the account of Rahab's preservation at Jericho; at least it emphasizes a different aspect of the ban than does the Rahab story (Josh. 6:22–25). In Joshua 9 the ban is perceived as an act of justice; its purpose is to ensure Israel a pure environment, free from the influences of polytheistic cults. In contrast, Joshua 6 presents the ban primarily as an act of sacrifice in which Israel devotes the firstfruits of Canaan to the Lord. Both views of the ban emphasize a response to God's action that ensures a proper stance before God. As a sacrifice, the ban represents an awareness of one's dependence on the Lord for victory in battle. As an expression of justice, it highlights the larger purpose of the torah to establish a worshiping community absolutely committed to the ideas of faith in God. In the stories of Rahab and the Gibeonites we see exceptions to the ban in all its purposes and nuances. Just as Rahab illustrates the possibility of a "devoted thing" being redeemed (Lev. 27:29), the Gibeonites show that an immediate neighbor of Israel could be preserved (Deut. 20:10–18).

Some have concluded that the stories of Rahab and the Gibeonites are primarily etiological; that is, their purpose is to explain some present reality (the presence of Canaanites who remain in the land) by means of stories from the past. Furthermore, on a literary level, these stories prepare the way for Judges 2—16, which narrates how the indigenous population of Canaan became a snare for Israel. The problem with this interpretation is that the text never indicates that these redeemed Canaanites (Rahab and the Gibeonites) pose any threat to Israel; on the contrary, they are viewed quite positively. Both Rahab and the Gibeonites acknowledge Israel's God as the supreme power, the creator and primary mover in the world. Their confessions of belief in God's might and their ultimate dependence on him for salvation are exemplary (Josh. 2:9–13; 9:9, 24). Therefore, it seems better to conclude that these stories are included not to explain the Canaanite survival in the land so much as to mitigate traditions about the ban. The qualification of the ban has a twofold impact on the larger conquest account: On the one hand, the present shape of the story suggests God's compassion to the Canaanites by showing that the Deuteronomic stipulation of their total destruction simply was not carried out, and Joshua is still held up as a model of torah faithfulness. Moreover, it shows that the purpose of the ban is not to keep ethnic purity by annihilating the Canaanites but to establish a society that has the Mosaic law at its center. On the other hand, the preservation of the Gibeonites and inclusion of them as temple servants highlights Israel's identity as a mixed multitude. These "outsiders" are not as atypical as is sometimes thought. Indeed, they represent many Israelites and, to judge from Joshua 9, a rather positive element within Israelite society. Perhaps those who recognize their precarious place before Israel's God, facing the ban and certain destruction, more readily acknowledge their dependence on God's mercy. But for whatever reason, the Gibeonites, like Rahab before them, are keenly aware of God's expectations as expressed in the Deuteronomic law, and they appropriately submit to the torah by gaining admission into the covenant community.

Identifying with the Underdog

As the preacher or teacher explores Joshua 9 for theological significance, appropriate questions might be, How does the church relate to characters like the Gibeonites? Are we sympathetic with their plight and glad to see them gain salvation, even by dishonest means, or do we begrudge their preservation because we perceive them as undeserving or dishonest? In other words, to whom is Joshua 9 good news? Many Christians relate to the Gibeonite story as they do to Jesus' parable of laborers in the vineyard (Matt. 20:1–16). They assume the Gibeonites, like the workers who come at the end of the day, have received something they do not deserve. The preacher might find it most helpful to turn that assumption on the congregation, to suggest that all who receive God's grace have been grafted in where they do not rightly belong. That identity with the underdog of the story would bring the church closer to Israel in its own self-understanding. In other words, empathizing with the Gibeonites probably helps the modern reader to receive the impact Joshua 9 had on ancient Israelites. The story undoubtedly pushed Israel to view the "outsiders" in its midst as integrally part of the community, sometimes modeling dependence on God for the rest. The story also connected to Israel's own extreme, sometimes dishonest efforts to preserve itself. This reading of Joshua 9 would perhaps also make more understandable the success of tricksters in the Old Testament and the surprising reversals in certain parables of Jesus (Matt. 20:1–16; Luke 16).

Joshua 10—12
The Land Rests from War

Joshua 11:23 concludes the story of Joshua's sweep of northern and southern territories by saying that "the land had rest from war." For most readers, however, those peaceful words are lost amidst the gruesome stories of Joshua slaughtering enemies, impaling kings, and burning cities. In fact, many know this section of Joshua through the alliterative and rhythmic English terms "fight" and "smite," which occur repeatedly in Joshua 10—12 in some older translations. It cannot be denied that these words appear numerous times in this section, along with other terms that refer to acts of war. Yet there are also signs in this section of the book that Joshua's authors were concerned about the issue of violence, much as modern readers are. Also largely unnoticed is that Joshua 10—12 presents important theological claims amidst its stories of warfare.

Joshua 10—12 is a collection of varied material, held together by the common theme of Joshua consolidating Israel's control over the land. The section begins with a report of Israel coming to Gibeon's aid when a group of southern kings form a coalition against it (10:1–14). At the center of this section are accounts of Joshua capturing southern (10:16–42) and northern territories (11:6–20) and executing the kings of the cities that rise against him there. Both of these subsections end with broad conclusions of how Joshua "took the whole land" (10:40–42;

89

11:16–23). Two prominent structural features tie chapters 10 and 11 together: First, Joshua 10:1–5 and 11:1–5 both report the Canaanite reaction to Israel, using very similar conventions of speech ("When king _____ heard . . . , he sent . . ."); these introductory segments are important because they cast the conquest of a majority of territory (save Jericho and Ai) as a result of Israel defending Gibeon out of covenant obligation. Second, at the end of both the Gibeonite story (10:14–15) and the report of Joshua's southern sweep (10:42–43), there is a two-part conclusion, stating that "the LORD fought for Israel" (10:14–15, 42–43) and that Joshua returned to Gilgal (10:15; 11:43). Chapter 12 then serves as a larger summary of the whole conquest, including the exploits of Moses east of the Jordan (12:1–6) and the actions of Joshua west of the river (12:7–24).

The Lord Fought for Israel (10:1–14)

Joshua 10:1–14 is intimately connected to the story of the Gibeonite covenant in chapter 9. On the basis of the treaty with Israel, the Gibeonites appealed to Joshua for military support when the king of Jerusalem led a force against them. Hence, the story in 10:1–14 is part of the larger account of the Gibeonite ruse. Joshua 10:1–5 is parallel to 9:1–2 in that it introduces the story by describing the Canaanite reaction to Israel's presence in the land. In 10:1–5 the king of Jerusalem plots against the city of Gibeon because of the covenant the Gibeonites established in chapter 9. The problem king Adoni-zedek has with the Gibeonite treaty is twofold: first, the successes of Joshua's army at Jericho and Ai made apparent that the Israelites would be quite a contentious force; second, Jerusalem's king undoubtedly realized that the Gibeonites, with their newly established treaty with Israel, were bound by oath to stand with Israel in any military action in the land. Therefore, for all practical purposes the Gibeonites had become enemies of their Canaanite neighbors. This was important because of Gibeon's military capability. According to verse 2, Gibeon was "a large city, like one of the royal cities, and was larger than Ai, and all its men were warriors." The delineation classifies Gibeon with the thirty-one cities listed in Joshua 12:9–24, each of which is identified by its king. Hence, Gibeon would have been an important part of an anti-Israelite coalition, had it not covenanted with Joshua and his army.

The primary point of 10:1–14, however, is not Israel's defense of the Gibeonites but God's intervention on behalf of Israel. Of course, we have seen this theme numerous times already in the book of Joshua, but Joshua 10:14 says the act of God was so extraordinary, that that day was

90

like no other day. Yet there are questions concerning the exact nature of God's action. The story reports that God acted in two ways. First, God threw "stones from heaven" on Israel's enemy (10:11). Some have naturally concluded this report was inspired by a fierce hailstorm that occurred during a battle. That may be the origin of the story, but the author makes specific claims about God's involvement that cannot be explained simply by natural phenomena. The icy balls are said to have killed more soldiers than the Israelites killed with the sword, but, even more amazing, the hail apparently killed no Israelites. The point is that the hail was the weapon of the divine warrior, fighting for Israel (see Job 38:22–23).

There are more questions and potential theological problems concerning the second claim, that the sun stopped and the moon ceased its course through the sky (10:13). The main theological issue is that, unless the Hebrew text is altered (with the assumption that it contains a mistake), verse 12b seems to depict Joshua addressing the heavenly bodies directly. This would have been inappropriate, since Israel's official religion denied that the sun and moon represented deities. Indeed, Genesis 1:16 simply calls them "greater and lesser lights" to avoid the temptation of thinking they were divine (as did Israel's neighbors), or that they represented Israel's God. But the theological difficulty is alleviated by two considerations: First, while it is true that Israel departed from its neighbors by refusing to worship the sun and moon, the Old Testament sometimes attributes to these objects the ability to praise the Lord (Ps. 148:3). It is possible that Joshua 10:12–13 assumes the sun and moon were part of God's heavenly court, fully under the suzerainty of the Lord but still having power to exert on his behalf. Second, verse 12a makes clear that Joshua spoke directly to the Lord. This itself does not remove the problem of the address in verse 12b, since it leaves open the possibility that Joshua thought of the sun and moon as manifestations of God. In verse 14, however, the editor of the story states that it was the Lord, not the sun or moon, who answered Joshua's prayer: "*[T]he* LORD heeded a human voice; for *the* LORD fought for Israel." Early interpreters highlighted this feature of the story and took Joshua 10:12–13 as a great testimony to the power of Joshua as a man of prayer (Sir. 46:1–6; Josephus, *Antiquities* 5.1.17).

There is also a question of what Joshua asks the sun and moon to do. The Hebrew term translated "stand still" (Hebrew root, *dmm*) can also mean, "be silent," which could imply that the heavenly lights were simply not visible (but the word applied to the moon, Hebrew *ʿmd*, more clearly means "stand"). In this case, verse 12 could refer either to an eclipse or to the sun being hidden because of fog or storm (note that

91

a hailstorm is mentioned in v. 11). Some of the awkwardness is no doubt created by the fact that the poetic line in verse 12b is taken from an ancient source, the book of Jashar, that may or may not have referred to this battle in its use of the line quoted (it is also not clear how much of v. 13a is part of the quote from the book of Jashar). Regardless of how one resolves these issues related to the sun standing still, the final form of the story again seems to answer our question. Verse 13b interprets verse 13a to mean that the sun (the moon is not mentioned in 13b) stopped in its course through the sky (as the ancients imagined it moving). The significance of the sun stopping may simply be that the daylight hours were lengthened so Joshua had more time to defeat the enemy. This would make sense, given that battles in the ancient Near East ceased at sunset. But the fact that the sun and moon are both mentioned requires further explanation. Some have suggested that the sun and moon appearing together constituted a positive omen. Indeed, some Assyrian astrological texts mention the visibility of two lights on the fourteenth day of the month as a positive sign that ensured success (see Holladay, "The Day[s] the Moon Stood Still," p. 176). But the point of Joshua 10:13 is not simply their appearance, but that the phenomenon continued for a time beyond what was expected. Habakkuk 3:10bβ–11 helps clarify the matter. It uses language similar to Joshua 10:12b–13 to say that the sun and moon stopped during a battle fought by God. In other words, these elements were under the Lord's control. They were not themselves deities that could act independently, as Israel's Canaanite opponents might have assumed; rather, they were instruments of the Lord's power exercised on behalf of Israel. Whatever the importance of the day being lengthened, the point of Joshua 10:12b–13 is not that Joshua received an omen (though knowledge of such signs may loom in the background of the passage) but that the Lord fought for Israel using the sun and moon as two of his implements (Miller, *The Divine Warrior in Early Israel*, pp. 26–127).

For some modern readers the truth claims of Joshua 10:12–14 are problematic. Indeed, our own worldview discourages us from affirming the historicity of stories of divine intervention. We tend to explain such accounts as the result of ancient misunderstandings of natural phenomena or as mythical accounts of divine activity. In short, the modern conception of reality does not permit the conclusion that "[t]here has been no day like it before or since, when the LORD heeded a human voice; for the LORD fought for Israel" (10:14). All days must be the same in the modern worldview, because modernity holds that the heavenly lights that define day and night are controlled by certain natural laws.

At stake in our interpretation of this text is nothing less than our view of God's role in history and nature. This does not mean that the details of Joshua 10:1–14 must be taken as historical in order to be faithful to Scripture. In fact, we must recognize that the notion of the sun standing still is not as unique as Joshua 10:14 indicates. There is a very similar story in the *Iliad* (II.412) in which Agamemnon prays that the sun would not set until the Achaeans won their battle. Hence, Joshua's authors are using battle imagery and descriptive language known in other traditions, and from that point one might conclude that the story in Joshua 10:1–14 is not historical. Nevertheless, that point should not end discussion of the larger issue, God's involvement in human affairs. Historicity may not have been the real issue for the author of this story, either. He is, after all, drawing information from an ancient source; he is not claiming to have seen the sun stand still. Rather, his main concern was that God could and did intervene within history for Israel. Herein lies the main issue for modern Christians. This author, like all biblical writers, thought of history and nature as parts of the created order that God controlled. He conceived humans as part of nature and therefore subject to the movements of history over which God was master. The modern view of things has radically changed these relationships so that humans are separate from nature, and humans shape history. This worldview encourages an understanding of God as one who allows the world to run by natural law and of humans as those who move and shape history. Joshua 10:1–14 calls the church to wrestle with this arrogant understanding of humanity. For indeed the church claims that there was a day like no other, namely the day of the resurrection of the Lord (Acts 2:29–36). That day was not brought about by human will or plan but by the act of God on behalf of broken humanity.

Royal Power Defeated (10:16—11:23)

Joshua 10:16—11:23 contains one of the most gruesome accounts in the book. It says Joshua swept through southern territories (10:16–43) and then northern areas (11:1–15) smiting, burning, and destroying everyone in the towns he encountered. But, as in many other parts of Joshua 1—12, there are signs that this report should not be read as a blow-by-blow historical account. The descriptions of Hebron (10:36–37) and Debir (10:38–39) provide prime illustrations of this point. Despite the fact that the account says Joshua utterly destroyed the residents of these two cities, they are mentioned again in 11:21 as though they had not been attacked, and later Hebron and Debir are given to Caleb to conquer (13:6–15; 15:15). These discrepancies in the

93

accounts force us to look for something other than historical fact as the motivation for their writing, though some historical memory may remain in the narrative. While that does not remove the violent descriptions from the story, there are theological points being made here in the story of Joshua's southern and northern campaigns (see pp. 95–96, "The Ethics of Revolution"). Namely, all the cities Joshua conquers are depicted, and later listed in chapter 12, as "royal cities." Gibeon was early on distinguished from these towns, even though it had similar military capability (10:2). What seems to be narrated in Joshua 10—11, therefore, is a repudiation and defeat of royal power. The problem is not monarchy itself, but a form of monarchy that is based on oppression. Some historians have proposed that Joshua 10—11 may have been inspired by a revolt of peasants against the powerful and greedy kings of Canaanite city-states and that the story of these peasants became incorporated into the story of the nation of Israel (Gottwald, *The Hebrew Bible*, pp. 272–76). Whether or not this specific interpretation is correct, the general idea of Joshua 10—11 as a repudiation of royal oppression is a key to the meaning of the Lord's order in 11:6 to burn the chariots and hamstring the horses that belong to these armies. These two parts of the military machine symbolized the application of royal hegemony, gained often through brutality and abuse. Hence, this account stands with many other texts in the Old Testament against monarchy's misuse of power and vaunting itself above all other authority (Deut. 17:14–20; 1 Kgs. 12:1–15). Hazor, the last town listed in the northern territory, is described as "the head of all those kingdoms" (11:10) and singled out for total destruction, like Jericho at the beginning of the conquest. It is difficult to say whether it was destroyed because it exemplified monarchical authority, or because it marked a northern counterpart to Jericho, or both. What is clear is that this section of the book testifies to the establishment of an egalitarian society, as outlined in the Mosaic torah, while simultaneously ridding the land of royal hierarchy (Deut. 17:14–20). To be sure, Israel's kings would often act out of their own self-interests, against the Lord's plan, like the kings defeated in Joshua 10—12. Nevertheless, the ideals presented in this story require those who object to its violence also to question other movements to establish a free society, including the American and French Revolutions.

Summary of Joshua's Success (11:16–23)

The summary verses at the end of chapter 11 mention twice that "Joshua took the whole land" (11:16, 23), securing the rest that was promised in 1:12–15. Joshua 11:16 concludes the entire conquest story in Joshua, and it serves as a parallel to 10:40, which speaks more narrowly of land conquered in the south. It is not clear, however, what "all the land" in 11:16 includes. The reference to Goshen is most confusing. This is the name of the area in Egypt where Joseph's family settled (Gen. 46:28–34), but it also is listed as a territory Israel captured in the south (Josh. 10:41) and later as a city belonging to Judah (Josh. 15:51). It is best understood as part of the southern territory, not as an area in Egypt. If that is the case, the description of the land in 11:16–17, along with 10:40, describes the farthest limits of the Davidic monarchy, an ideal set of borders for an author in the time of Josiah, when some of the territory was being reclaimed, or in the exile, when the people hoped to regain Canaan and revive the nation's former glory.

The Ethics of Revolution

Joshua 10—12 raises daunting ethical questions for the church, just as many other portions of the book have as well (see the commentary on Josh. 2; 5:13—6:27; 7:1—8:29; 9). Again, the most troubling feature of these chapters is the issue of the ban. Although the subject arises in other parts of the book and the ban is said to be applied completely at Jericho, chapters 10—12 have by far the most concentrated discussion of the Canaanites being "utterly destroyed." Adding to this horrific portrait the hamstringing of horses, one finds enough record of abuse in these chapters to repulse any modern person of faith. And yet, as we have observed in other sections of the book, there are redeeming qualities in this section and even attractive theological concerns for the contemporary reader. As we have already noted, this point is possible in part because Joshua 10—12 does not present a historically accurate picture of a conquest in the late Bronze Age (1550–1200 B.C.), the time of Joshua. The sweep of territories may reflect the campaigns of Josiah, the king at the time Joshua began to be written, or it was possibly influenced by David's control over the land. Regardless of what influenced the present story, it is clear that Joshua 10—12 is a theological history and must be read for its theological significance first and foremost.

As noted earlier, this section of the book makes a strong statement against the kind of royal power that Deuteronomy also speaks against. The law concerning the king in Deuteronomy 17:14–20 specifically prohibits acquiring many horses (v. 16), which refers to a large professional army (see 1 Sam. 8:11; 1 Kgs. 10:26). Therefore, the Lord's order to burn all chariots and hamstring all horses is connected to the Deuteronomic ideal for life in Canaan, and Israel's action is depicted as a battle to make that ideal a reality (11:6; cf. 11:9). While the hamstringing of horses is certainly cruelty to animals, it must be taken in the context of a world in which the horse was used in a system of weaponry. This animal was as essential to military tactics as the tank or bomber today and was used to bring as much terror as any modern implement of war.

Still, the greatest problem in this section of the book, as in previous chapters, is the notion that Joshua "utterly destroyed" the residents of all the towns on his campaign. In the case of Joshua 10—11, the offense is lessened somewhat by the identification of each town with its king. In Joshua 10:16–27, five kings are captured and impaled, and then Joshua proceeds to attack each of their towns. In every other case the emphasis is on the king of the city (such as at Debir in 10:38–39), and with Hazor the accent is particularly on the town being head of the surrounding kingdoms. But these chapters show even further that there is a concern for how the conquest is presented. Violence is an issue for the authors, as we see in Joshua 10:1–5 and 11:1–5. These sections place Joshua's conquest in a context that frames the action as a response to the aggressiveness of the kings in Canaan. In 10:1–5 the southern kings form an alliance against Gibeon, which Israel is bound by covenant to defend. Then 11:1–5 portrays the northern kings as a great fighting force, "in number like the sand on the seashore, with very many horses and chariots" (v. 4), gathered to fight against Israel. Hence the conquest almost becomes a defensive action, as Joshua responds to the threat of these royal cities. This is underscored by Joshua 11:19, which states that not a single city made peace with Israel, except Gibeon. It sounds as though the kings and their cities did not have to be destroyed. If they had only acted like Rahab and the Gibeonites, their fate would have been different (Stone, "Ethical and Apologetic Tendencies," p. 33). Joshua 11:20 ties the conquest of these kings to Israel's experience in Egypt when Pharaoh's heart was hardened (see Deut. 7:1–2). As in the exodus story, the hardening motif appears only after a record that the kings failed to recognize the Lord's control over the land. Therefore, when Joshua 10—12 is read as a theological narrative, it accentuates God's graciousness to Israel and God's desire to be compassionate to the Canaanites as well. But the Canaanite kings refused to acknowledge God's authority and thereby missed their opportunity for God's grace. The harsh treatment of Canaanite kings and their people should be understood as part of an ethic of revolution. Revolution often brings death and destruction for those whose outmoded or oppressive practices stand in the way of new visions for life and governance. Israel's conquest is depicted as such a revolutionary movement, called for and informed by the torah of Moses.

PART TWO

Dividing the Land
for an Inheritance

JOSHUA 13—22

Joshua 13—22 is undoubtedly the most neglected portion of the book. This is in part because to many readers the extensive lists of towns and territories in this section seem as empty theologically as the genealogies in Genesis or lists of temple singers in Chronicles (a judgment that itself is misguided, though it is a common one). The failure to pay attention to these chapters is also due to the common judgment that they are later additions to the book, arising largely from priestly interests during and after the exile. The latter point has become commonplace in scholarly discussions. Indeed, many interpreters have seen the setting of land allotment in Joshua's old age as a sign of late insertion (13:1). The line in Joshua 13:1 seems to imitate 23:1b, where the phrase "Joshua was old and advanced in years" is more natural as an introduction to Joshua's farewell speech (see the similar introduction to Samuel's final words in 1 Sam. 12:2; cf. 1 Kgs. 1:1; but see an alternate view of the matter in Auld, *Joshua, Moses, and the Land*, pp. 52–56). Despite the logic of that argument, however, Joshua 13—22 fits naturally into the book and forms an essential part of its message. Joshua 11:23 presented two roles for Joshua, first, to take the land and, second, to "give it for an inheritance to Israel according to their tribal allotments." Chapters 13—22 expand on that verse and portray Joshua in his second, if less famous, role as Moses' successor.

This section has a very important but seldom appreciated theological role in the book and in the Old Testament. Indeed, Joshua 13—22 has profound implications for Israel's establishment of a just society, according the ideals of the Mosaic torah. The distribution of land emphasizes that Canaan is apportioned for the good of all Israel,

97

not just for a privileged few. In turn, this portrait of land distribution is formative for Israel's self-understanding as a covenant community. Prophets like Isaiah and Micah express a concern for the maintenance of this self-understanding. They denounce capitalist-style profiteers who "covet fields, and seize them," (Micah 2:2), joining "house to house" (Isa. 5:8). What they rail against is precisely the practice of some wealthy citizens who seize property that, for the poor, represents membership in the covenant community (see the larger discussion of Mays, "Justice: Perspectives from the Prophetic Tradition," pp. 10–11). Joshua 13—22 is guided by a theology of land possession that was supposed to structure Israel's common life in Canaan. The land allotments were to be an inheritance (Hebrew *nahalah*), land kept within families and passed on to future generations as a sign of relationship to the covenant-making God. Although it is not certain if this section of the book existed in written form during the ministry of the eighth-century prophets, in the present shape of the prophetic corpus of the canon, Joshua 13—22 is the foundation upon which they stand.

These chapters carry yet another message for the audiences addressed by the final form of Joshua, particularly those Israelites living during the age of restoration (after 539 B.C.). During this time the Jordan became a definitive border between Israelite and non-Israelite territory, as Ezekiel 47:13—48:29 attests (see especially Ezek. 47:18; this delineation of borders could be earlier than Ezek. 47, but this is not certain). Land east of the river was considered unclean, a notion that gave rise to questions about whether or not residents of those areas could participate in Israel's worship and, indeed, whether or not they were really Israelite. Probably for that reason, this section of Joshua pays much attention to the tribes who live east of the Jordan (13:8–31; 22). As Dennis Olson notes, the land they occupy is "a place of fuzzy borders, an in-between land not fully part of the promised land, yet settled by Israelite tribes" (*Numbers*, p. 188). In the end there is a judgment for unity. Whether east or west of the Jordan, the most important mark of inclusion in the cultic community is the confession of the Lord as the only God, not the land the people occupy. This issue of unity in the worshiping community frames chapters 13—22 and attests to the topic's central importance in ancient Israel. Given that emphasis, the church today, with its constant infighting over the nature of purity and questions of who is or is not fit to minister or be part of the community, should pay heed to this often overlooked portion of Joshua.

Joshua 13:1–7
The Lord Gives, the Lord Assigns by Lot

The second major portion of the book of Joshua opens with a speech in which God instructs Joshua concerning the task of allotting the land to Israel. It begins with the Lord restating in verse 1b what the narrator communicated in verse 1a, that Joshua "was old and advanced in years." Stylistically, this parallels the opening of the book, in which the narrator's reference to the death of Moses in 1:1a is repeated by God in 1:1b. The similarity in structure in these two beginnings indicates that the conquest and apportionment of the land are both essential to Joshua's commissioning as Moses' successor. After the initial statement about Joshua's advanced age, the Lord declares that "much of the land still remains to be possessed" (v. 1b) and lists areas yet unconquered. As we have already observed, this description of territory still in Canaanite control is in tension with Joshua 11:16 and 23, which say that Joshua "took the whole land." But the claim of how Israel will eventually possess Canaan made in 13:1–7 is essentially the same as that made in Joshua 1:1–9. In Joshua 13:6 the Lord says, "I will myself drive them out." The term rendered here as "drive out" is the same Hebrew word, in different form, as that translated "possess" in verse 1 (Hebrew *yaraš*). In other words, Israel will possess the land (v. 1) because the Lord will dispossess the Canaanites (v. 6). Therefore, it is wrong to contrast Joshua 1—12 as a theological account of how God *gave* the land with Joshua 13—22 as a more historical portrait of how Israel *took* Canaan. Both portions of the book declare that the land is God's gift. This is reinforced by God's instructions to Joshua in 13:6b. When the Lord tells him to "allot" the land, he uses a term meaning "to let fall" (Hebrew *napal*) that often appears in the context of casting lots (Neh. 10:34). As we shall see in Joshua 14:1, this is exactly how the land was divided. The lot was an implement cast, and then "read," in order to receive directions from God. By this means Joshua determined Achan's guilt in Joshua 7:14, and later in Israel's history the first king is selected by casting lots (1 Sam. 10:16–26). Hence, even the assignment of certain areas to particular tribal groups was due to the Lord's action.

Joshua 13:8–33
Inheritance Received from Moses

The tribes of the Transjordan are dealt with first, after the Lord's instructions to Joshua. Reuben, Gad, and the half-tribe of Manasseh were highlighted in Joshua's installation in chapter 1, and they will be prominent again in chapter 22, evidence of their great importance for issues of national unity. Joshua 13:8–33 divides naturally into four smaller units: 13:8–14, a general description of the territory given to the two and a half tribes east of the Jordan, points back to Moses as the one who assigned their territories and towns and ends with a note that Moses gave no inheritance to the Levites, a reference that occurs again in 13:33; then, 13:15–23, 24–28, and 29–33 list the land and towns occupied by Reuben, Gad, and the half-tribe of Manasseh respectively.

This section basically repeats what Moses reported in Deuteronomy 3:8–22, which is also laid out in Numbers 32:1—34:15. There is no talk of casting lots to determine the land divisions east of the Jordan in any of these accounts, nor is the term "to let fall" used (as it was in Josh. 13:6). This has led some scholars to conclude that the eastern territory was considered inferior, perhaps not officially a part of the promised land (see Josh. 22:19). The story in Numbers does say that the Lord gave this land to Israel when he delivered Sihon and Og to them (Num. 21:34), and Deuteronomy 3:18 likewise states that Transjordan is a divine gift. But, as we shall see in Joshua 22, the allotments of Reuben, Gad, and half-Manasseh raise questions of national unity that reflect some ambiguity over this territory.

Joshua 14—19
Canaan Distributed by Lot

Joshua 14:1–5 introduces the allotments west of the river with three pieces of information that are essential for understanding the apportionment of the land: First, the priest, Eleazar, who helped commission Joshua in Numbers 27:21 (and there is named as keeper of the sacred lots), shares the duty of assigning the land, as do the "heads of the families of the tribes" as well. Therefore, the process is democratic, as far as human involvement goes, and reflects the radical concern for inclusion and equality. Second, the land is apportioned by lot, as Joshua 14:2 indicates. Although the Hebrew term for this object, *goral*, recurs throughout the rest of the report of the allotment west of the river (15:1; 16:1; 17:1, 21:8), the Greek version has a term meaning "boundary" in these subsequent references. This may indicate that the original reading in Hebrew actually had the similar term, *gĕbûl* (the difference in Hebrew being only one letter), meaning "boundary" or "border," which would make sense in each case. Regardless of which reading is correct, the mention of the lot in Joshua 14:2 still makes clear that Joshua and Eleazar meted out the land according to divine instructions. Third, the text explains that Joseph was divided into two tribes, Manasseh and Ephraim, but that the Levites did not receive an inheritance of land; thus the number of tribal groups receiving allotments remained at twelve, the perfect number.

Among the tribes west of the Jordan, Judah takes priority. Their territorial allotment is described from Joshua 14:6 to the end of chapter 15. A prominent part of the treatment of Judah is the account of Caleb, who requests and is granted possession of Hebron in 14:6–15, and then occupies it in 15:13–19. In Joshua 14:6b–12 Caleb gives an impassioned speech in which he declares his full devotion to God and presents himself as an exemplary devotee of the Lord who will fight the Lord's battles. The speech contains allusions to texts in Deuteronomy, particularly Deuteronomy 9:1–2 in which Moses promises that God will drive out the Anakim, a race of giants, produced by the union of divine beings and humans (Gen. 6:4; Num. 13:33). Caleb puts himself forward as the one through whom God can rid the land of the Anakim, to fulfill the promise that came through Moses. Hence, Caleb appears as a man of faith and courage, zealously committed to the Lord's cause. That makes quite interesting the way he is introduced: his lineage indicates he is the son of a foreigner, a Kenizzite. With this introduction, Caleb, like Rahab, professes faith in an ideal way, even though his heritage is not pure. It increases the sense that the "outsiders" in Israel's midst often are ironically more insightful and more zealous for the Lord than are the pedigreed Israelites.

Richard Nelson classifies the account of Caleb as a particular type of story that occurs four other times in this section on the distribution of the land (15:18–19; 17:3–6, 14–18; 21:1–3). He calls it a "land grant narrative" because each example features (1) a lead character or characters making a case that land should be given, (2) an appeal to a prior agreement with Moses, and (3) a record that the land is granted (*Joshua*, p. 177; see his discussion for a more complete list of features).

The main characters in each of these stories show a certain degree of chutzpah in making their case; two of the stories involve women, who did not normally inherit property in the ancient Near East. The first is Caleb's daughter, Achsah (15:18–19). She asks her father for a piece of land as well as springs of water, and he gives her what she requests (see Judg. 1:11–15). Her gifts are not labeled "inheritance," but the property granted to the daughters of Zelophehad in 17:3–6 is. Zelophehad is said to have had no sons, only daughters. So the daughters sought an inheritance alongside their male relatives in the tribe of Manasseh. It would be anachronistic to say that the narrative shows a concern for equality or equal rights. But it does testify strongly to the concern for all Israelites to have a share in the promises God made to Abraham. Since the daughters of Zelophehad had no brothers, their family heritage could not be carried on in the land unless they were granted an inheritance on their father's behalf to pass on to their children.

Two additional notes on Judah's allotment seem important. First, the outline of their territory in 15:1–12 is carefully drawn so as to exclude Jerusalem. This no doubt assumes that Jerusalem was not an Israelite city until David captured it and made it his capital (2 Sam. 5:6–15; but see Judg. 1:8). Second, the list of Judah's towns in 15:20–63 is curious. Most of the list follows a pattern in which a group of settlements in a particular area are named, and then there is a summary statement that gives the number of those towns. This pattern is broken in verses 45–47, which highlight three towns along the Mediterranean coast, Ekron, Ashdod, and Gaza. Each town is mentioned singularly so that it stands out from the rest of the larger town list. In addition to this break in form, one wonders why Ashkelon is not mentioned here, since it was perhaps the most prominent city in this region. The answer seems to lie in the message Joshua's authors were trying to make about Israel's relationship to the other nations. Ekron, Ashdod, and Gaza were Assyrian administrative centers, towns populated and controlled by Assyrian officials during their dominance of Israel's land in the eighth and seventh centuries B.C. By listing these three towns as Judah's, as they appear in Assyrian administrative documents, Joshua's authors seem to be saying what they have said already in the book, that Israel is not the property or under the control of any foreign power (Josh. 1:4). The Lord controls the land and gives it to Israel as its inheritance.

After the allotments of the Joseph tribes in chapters 16 and 17 (Ephraim in chap. 16 and the other half of Manasseh in chap. 17), the rest of the tribes are treated in Joshua 18—19. The land of Judah and Joseph was apportioned at Gilgal (14:6), but now the location shifts to Shiloh (18:1). Despite the change of place, however, the portrait of

102

national unity and divine allotment continue in this final section. The tribes who have already received their portion have not departed. Rather, "the whole congregation of the Israelites assembled" (18:1). Reference to the tent of meeting ensures the reader that God is governing these allotments, like those in chapters 14—17. In 18:6 we also read that the territories of the remaining tribes are assigned by lot, as were the earlier assignments for Judah and the Joseph groups. The land division concludes with Joshua receiving his own town, Timnath-serah, as Caleb received his (19:49–50). Joshua 19:51 gives a final reminder that Joshua and Eleazar had distributed Canaan by lot, further emphasizing that the division of the land was determined by God.

Joshua 20—21
Special Allotments for the Sake of Justice

The final allotments concern individual cities, located within territories already assigned to some of the tribes, that are set apart to meet the needs of persons whose citizen status has a certain ambiguity. Joshua 20 designates some cities as places of refuge for those who have killed another person under such circumstances that the killing was not considered a capital crime. The cities of refuge are discussed also in Exodus 21:13; Numbers 35:9–15; Deuteronomy 4:41–43; 19:1–13; and 1 Chronicles 6:54–81. The overarching concern of these texts and Joshua 20 is the shedding of innocent blood. That point may surprise some readers in light of the extensive description of Canaanites being "utterly destroyed" in chapters 2, 6, 8, and 10—11. It is another sign, however, that the purpose of the conquest of Canaan, as presented in Joshua, was to establish justice in the land as well as to supply Israel a homeland. As we have already noted, it may be helpful to distinguish between an ethic of revolution (see pp. 95–96, "The Ethics of Revolution"), which might involve killing innocent people, and a system of justice and righteousness that was meant to establish order and promote equity for Israel's life in the land.

The identification of these towns, and the need for them, is tied to specific ancient Near Eastern assumptions about murder and the punishment for it, ideas that may seem strange to modern readers. At the core of Joshua 20 is the notion that the spilling of blood (which was understood in an almost magical sense as representative of life) by murder brought an imbalance (as well as an injustice) to the created order.

103

It effected a kind of curse on the land (Deut. 19:10). As Numbers 35:33 states, "blood pollutes the land." Bloodguilt could be averted, it was believed, by the action of an "avenger of blood," an individual designated by the family of the dead person to seek "revenge" in the case of homicide (the avenger was probably the nearest relative to the deceased). To understand the concept further, it is important to recognize that the English "avenger" translates the Hebrew term, *goel*, which more properly means "redeemer" (Ruth 2:20; 3:13). Hence, the avenger was thought to "redeem" the blood of the dead relative, spilled where and in a manner that was not proper, by shedding the blood of the murderer. Again, as Numbers 35:33 states, in the case of the land being polluted by blood, "no expiation can be made for the land . . . except by the blood of the one who shed it." The practice of avenging a murder was so deeply ingrained in the Israelite psyche that it was institutionalized (Deut. 19:12). It was recognized, however, that homicide occurred sometimes under circumstances that were not clearly premeditated and, therefore, did not warrant avenging (Num. 35:22–24). In fact, if the avenger took the life of someone who had killed by accident, that act of retaliation itself would amount to shedding innocent blood and, therefore, perpetuate bloodguilt (again, see Deut. 19:10). In terms of modern justice, the cases exempted from the avenger would be classified as manslaughter or perhaps third-degree murder. Deuteronomy 19:4–5 provides a classic example: two men go into the forest to cut wood; the axe head belonging to one man slips and kills the other; if there was no previous enmity between the men, the case might be judged an accident, and the killer would be entitled to protection from the avenger of the dead man's family (see further, Num. 35:22–24).

Like so many other aspects of Joshua's leadership, this allotment of refuge cities follows the guidelines of Moses in Deuteronomy (Deut. 19:1–13). The identity of the cities seems to be motivated by consideration for even geographical distribution. Three cities were named east of the Jordan (Golan, Ramoth, and Bezer) and three west of the river (Kedesh, Shechem, and Hebron); in both cases cities were located in northern, central, and southern regions. The particular place of asylum in each of these cities may have been a sanctuary in which the person was thought to be protected by God's "shelter" at the altar (see an expression of the general idea, though perhaps not the specific notion of refuge from an avenger, in Ps. 61:1–4). Indeed, Exodus 21:13 implies that a sanctuary is the site of refuge when it notes that a person who kills another by accident should be given refuge, but one who "willfully attacks and kills another" should be taken from the altar for execution. Whether or not Joshua 20 has a sanctuary in mind is not certain, but the initial procedure for the one seeking refuge is clear, and Joshua 20:4–5 is somewhat unique in this detail: the slayer is to appear before the elders of the refuge city; they decide whether the person deserves asylum; if so, they are responsible for protecting the man from the avenger who pursues him (compare Deut. 19:12, which speaks of the elders of the town from which the killer has come; see Num. 35:24). Verse 6 includes another provision of uncertain meaning, namely, that at the death of the high priest at the time of the murder, the slayer could return to his home. This loophole for the manslayer is emphasized in Numbers 35:25, 28, 32. It probably reflects an extension of amnesty offered when a high priest died. Moreover, it also indicates that the action of the avenger of blood was not primarily for retaliation (though that may have motivated him as well); rather, the death of a murderer was to purify the land of bloodguilt. Put another way, revenge for murder served a ritual purpose and was, therefore, institutionalized; by the same token, the murder that brought bloodguilt seems to have been pardoned at times, times when revenge became unacceptable.

Joshua 21 makes special allowances for a second ambiguous group in Israel, the Levites. As we have seen already, there is a strong interest in this tribe in Joshua 13—22. The Levites had the Lord as their portion, so they did not possess territory. Their inheritance came through their service in the sanctuary or later in the temple. They did have need, however, for lodging and a place to pasture their flocks. Thus, certain cities were reserved for these purposes. It should be noted further that the cities of refuge, listed in chapter 20, are also identified as Levitical towns in chapter 21. Hence, the Levites may have overseen or played a prominent role in the institution of asylum for the one who killed unintentionally.

Joshua 22
The Problem of Unity

Joshua 21 ends with a glorious conclusion about the allotment of land to Israel, similar to the idealistic summary in 11:23: "Not one of all the good promises that the LORD had made to the house of Israel had failed; all came to pass" (21:45). Chapter 22 is connected to the section that precedes it by the common interest in "rest" that was achieved as a result of the apportionment of land (21:44; 22:4). While Israel had rest from their Canaanite enemies, however, the story in Joshua 22 shows

105

that they discovered an even greater adversary—themselves! This narrative raises key questions about the place of the three Transjordan tribes in the cultic community. These Israelite groups get attention in the book at three key places of beginning, ending, or transition (1:12–18; 13:8–33; 22:1–34). Therefore, their appearance in chapter 22 is important for the structure and theology of Joshua as a whole. It shows that the entire book is shaped around concerns regarding these tribes, namely, concerns over the unity of Israel and the inclusion of the territory east of the Jordan in Israel's inheritance.

Scholars often note that chapter 22 was created from at least two sources, one Deuteronomistic (vv. 1–6) and the other Priestly (vv. 9–34), with verses 7–8 serving as the glue to hold them together. The division into sources is seen in part by the shift in lead characters: Joshua, who dominates verses 1–6, disappears completely in verses 9–34, where Phinehas, the ideal priest remembered for his stemming of the Peor sin in Numbers 25, enters as the main character. While the logic of this source division is easy enough to see, a focus on the development of the chapter from these sources misses the rather unified story that comes from their combination. Whatever its sources, the chapter works as a single narrative. This commentary will focus on three aspects of the story: the place of Joshua 22 in the book, the literary structure of the chapter, and the multiple theological interests that emerge from the concern with Israel's unity.

Chapter 22 in the Book of Joshua

Joshua 22 has important connections to portions of the book that precede and follow it, showing the centrality of the problem of tribal unity. Joshua's address (vv. 2–5) points forward to two other speeches Joshua gives before his death. Although each of the three addresses has its own emphases and unique setting and structure, they are nonetheless united by a common admonition to obey the torah of Moses (22:5; 23:6; 24:25–27). Furthermore, when Joshua sends the Transjordan tribes to their inheritance in 22:6, it anticipates his doing the same for the whole nation in 24:28. But Joshua 22:1–5 also recalls subjects in chapter 1: in 22:5 Joshua charges the eastern tribes to obey the torah of Moses as he did also in 1:13 (cf. 1:7–8); in 22:2–3 he praises them for supporting their kindred, in fulfillment of his command in 1:13–15; in 22:4 Joshua grants the Transjordan tribes the rest they were promised in 1:13. Hence, chapter 22 closes the file, as it were, on the tribes of Reuben, Gad, and the half-tribe of Manasseh, a file that has been open and has received much attention since the beginning of the book of Joshua.

The Structure of the Story

The chapter divides neatly into three sections. The first, verses 1–6, records Joshua's speech (vv. 2–5) after an introduction (v. 1) and before a narrative conclusion (v. 6). The speech itself consists of three parts: In verses 2–3 Joshua endorses the eastern tribes' faithfulness to the task of supporting the other tribes in their bid to win their territorial allotments. The affirmation of their deeds is ordered in verse 2 by verb pairs, "you observed" and "you obeyed" (literally "you heeded"), that describe the action of the eastern tribes. The objects of these verbs are expressed in two clauses, both of which include the verb "command" and the adverb "all" ("all Moses commanded" and "all I commanded"). Verse 3a expresses specifically what these tribes kept or obeyed by stating it negatively: "[Y]ou have not forsaken your kindred." The affirmation of the eastern groups concludes in verse 3b with another commendation that is general, but emphatic: "[You] have been careful to keep the charge of the LORD your God." Following this confirmation of their faithfulness, Joshua commands the eastern tribes to receive their rest (v. 4). Then the speech concludes with a charge to faithful observance of torah (v. 5), repeating much of the language of verse 2 ("observe," "command"). The carefully ordered language of the speech draws from the vocabulary and reflects the concerns of the book of Deuteronomy. This is particularly evident in Joshua's admonition to serve God "with all your heart and with all your soul," language found in the famous injunction in Deuteronomy 6:5.

Verses 7–9 make up a second division of the chapter (note the division suggested here does not follow the delimitation of sources discussed above). This section contains comments that help link verses 1–6 with verses 10–34. The transitional verses explain the fact that Manasseh is divided in two, with half the tribe settling east of the Jordan and the other half west of the river. The explication of the matter at this juncture seems unnecessary, since Joshua 22 presupposes a knowledge of the previous account of land allotment, as well as the tribal partitions laid out in Deuteronomy 3:12–22. It serves to emphasize, through the bifurcated Manasseh group, that those east of the river have an equal share in the inheritance promised to Israel. This statement of unity is communicated also, albeit more subtly, in the final note in verse 9 that the eastern tribes obtained their land through Moses (see also Deut. 3:8–22). Such information dispels ahead of time verse 19's idea concerning the eastern land's uncleanness.

The final portion of the story, verses 10–34, assuming the two previous sections, reports that the Reubenites, Gadites, and half-Manasseh group returned to their land and constructed an altar on the frontier between the eastern and western tribes, an act that raised the ire of their kindred. Verses 10–34 are structured so that the proximate center of the account, verses 21–29, presents the central theological subject, namely, why the eastern tribes' altar should not offend their kindred and why they built it in the first place (see Nelson, *Joshua*, p. 251).

Joshua's Authority (vv. 1–6)

The authority of Joshua is an implied subtheme in this section of material. The interest in Israel's unity in Joshua 22 begins with Joshua's speech to the eastern tribes in verses 2–5. In some ways Joshua's speech presents no surprises; as in other texts, Joshua defers to the authority of Moses and the Mosaic commandments (1:12–15). The high view of Moses is evident in the three occurrences of Moses' name accompanied by the common title "the servant of the Lord" (vv. 2, 4, 5). Moreover, Joshua utilizes some of the words of Moses in his own instructions, giving further attention to Moses' authority (v. 5; Deut. 6:5). But two new elements jar the reader out of the comfort created by the references to Moses. First, when Joshua commends the Transjordan tribes for their faithfulness he states, "You have observed all that Moses the servant of the LORD commanded" and *"have obeyed me* in all that I have commanded you" (v. 2). This paired reference to the commands of Moses and Joshua puts Joshua on a footing almost equal to Moses. Second, Joshua's blessing of the eastern tribes in verse 6 shows him in the same role as Moses when he blessed the Israelites at the close of his life in Deuteronomy 33. Hence Joshua 22:1–6 depicts Joshua as a fully endowed successor to Moses, with Moses-like authority. That also makes even more curious, however, the fact that Phinehas instead of Joshua appears in this chapter as the mediator of the conflict among the tribes. As with the tribal allotments in chapters 13—21, Joshua shares authority with a priest (see how Moses is also paired with Phinehas in Numbers 25, though not as clearly sharing authority). Regardless of the editorial history behind Joshua 22 and possible Priestly interests that gave the chapter its present shape, the impact on the reader is this: Joshua's power, which reaches a zenith in 22:1–6, is checked by the priestly authority of Phinehas. It perhaps suggests that the period of Moses and Moses' leadership was unique (as Deut. 34 says). No leader after Moses is able to fill his shoes and exercise complete authority. So, while the Mosaic typology implies Joshua's high status, it also subordinates him to Moses.

The Altar of Witness (vv. 10–34)

108

The conflict among the Israelites reported in verses 10–34 centers on the Transjordan tribes' building an altar by the Jordan. There are subtle hints in the story, however, that there is some other, more inherent split in the Israelite nation before the altar is constructed. To this point in the narrative, the first two eastern groups have been described with distinctive Hebrew titles (characteristic of Deuteronomistic literature) that sound like the titles in modern translations: Reubenites (Hebrew *rûbēnî*) and Gadites (Hebrew *gāddî*; v. 1). But curiously, the labels used for them in Hebrew change in verse 9 to "sons of Reuben" and "sons of Gad" (and similarly in v. 30 the half Manasseh group is called "sons of Manasseh"). Although English translations continue to render these titles in verses 9–34 the same as in verse 1, the difference in Hebrew is striking. This linguistic shift indicates that the two sources from which chapter 22 was composed used different vocabulary and style (note the same style, "sons of," in Joshua 4:12), but the variation has a profound impact on the final narrative. Indeed, the fact that the title given to the nation as a whole reads woodenly as "sons of Israel" (translated by NRSV as "Israelites") gives the impression that the "sons of Reuben," "sons of Gad," and "sons of Manasseh" represent some cultic and political entity that is separate from the rest of the nation. The titles seem to suggest a split that is not evident elsewhere. Furthermore, verse 11 states that the three eastern groups built an altar "on the side that belongs to the Israelites." The context suggests that this means they built the altar on the Canaan side of the Jordan. But does the other side of the Jordan, the side occupied by Reuben, Gad, and half Manasseh, not also belong to "the Israelites"? The ambiguity over who is Israelite and who is not is important, since the eastern groups express fear that one day they will not be considered "sons of Israel." The titles of the tribal groups give some hint of justification for their fears. Another subtle suggestion of disunity is Phinehas's statement about the land east of the Jordan being unclean (v. 19). The comment receives no more attention, but it adds to the impression that the eastern groups are not equal to the rest and must barter for a continued place in the covenant community. As we have already observed, these features of the narrative reflect a time, perhaps during the postexilic restoration, when the territory east of the Jordan was considered non-Israelite (see the commentary at the beginning of Part 2, pp. 97–98). Therefore, the land occupied by the eastern tribes seems to be at the heart of the problem in Joshua 22.

These hints of existing fractures within the Israelite people set the stage for the construction of the altar by the Jordan and the ensuing conflict over it. There are two essential issues that must be dealt with: First, why was the construction of an altar so grievous an offense that the Israelites would make war with their kindred over it? Second, why

109

might the building of the altar cause God's wrath toward the whole nation? Regarding the first question, although it is not stated explicitly, this story probably assumes regulations about worship found in Deuteronomy. Behind the concern here seems to be the prohibition of worshiping at any site except "the place that the LORD your God will choose out of all your tribes as his habitation to put his name there" (Deut. 12:5; compare Exod. 20:24, which speaks of multiple altars). Although this particular Deuteronomic law most precisely prohibits worship at former Canaanite sanctuaries, the larger concern for a central place of worship applies here as well. This interpretation is supported by two points in the story: (1) Phinehas emphasizes that a single altar is permitted for the nation, and that worship take place only there (22:19); (2) the western tribes raise their concern over the altar while gathered at Shiloh. Since Shiloh was the first place identified as the dwelling place of the Lord's name (Jer. 7:12), the Israelite presence at this place draws attention to the Deuteronomic law. It is also possible that the interest in a single place of sacrifice springs from Priestly interests, since the reference to the tabernacle in verse 29 is likely from that tradition. Moreover, the comparison of this altar to the sin in Numbers 25 may indicate a Priestly writer is at work, but the concern itself is more important for the story than its origin. There is one place approved for Israel's sacrifices, and the eastern tribes are suspected of breaking that regulation.

The offense committed by the eastern groups had religious as well as political connotations. The construction of an altar in a place other than at the central sanctuary was a breach of purity, and it could also be a declaration of independence, as Jeroboam's construction of altars at Bethel and Dan make clear (1 Kgs. 12:25–33). Both possible implications are expressed in verse 19: Phinehas orders the eastern tribes not to rebel against the Lord (a break in religious purity) and not to rebel "against us" (a sign of political confrontation).

The second essential question, about why the altar might cause the wrath of God to descend upon the whole nation, is answered indirectly within the narrative itself. Phinehas compares the altar to two sins in Israel's past: first, the episode at Peor (Num. 25), in which he himself eradicates the camp of foreign influences, and, second, Achan's stealing some of the devoted things from Jericho (Josh. 7). Although these two acts of disobedience are very different in character, they share a common response from God. In both cases a plaguelike event comes, or is feared to come, as the result of the sin. In both cases the sin is understood as creating a spiritual infection that threatens to wipe out

110

the whole community. These stories show that the sin of one Israelite brings guilt upon the whole nation, and Phinehas fears the same result from the altar built by the Jordan (see pp. 68–76, commentary on Josh. 7). An alternate translation of the last part of verse 19 communicates this fear further. Instead of reading, do not "rebel against us," the line could read, "do not make rebels of us." If that translation is adopted, it would add to the impression that the rebellion of one person or group brought guilt to all Israel. Such an understanding of verse 19 would place additional emphasis on the problem of the land. If the issue of the altar is that it makes the *whole* nation apostate, then there is a presumption that the eastern tribes themselves are integral to Israel. The greatest problem is not a division among the tribes themselves, but the land occupied by Reuben, Gad, and half of Manasseh.

The story suggests that the heart of the issue is apostasy, such as Moses warned against in Deuteronomy 13:12–18. In compliance with Moses' instructions, Phinehas leads a judicial process to determine if indeed the eastern tribes are guilty of such an offense. If found culpable, they would be destroyed, just as Achan was executed for his rebellion (Deut. 13:15). The Reubenites, Gadites, and half-tribe of Manasseh, however, convince the priest of their innocence.

The eastern tribes respond to Phinehas that the altar was not for sacrifice; rather it was a "copy" of an altar (v. 28). The word rendered "copy" might better be translated "pattern" or "model." Second Kings 16:10 uses the same word to refer to the model of an altar king Ahaz sent to the priest Uriah to be used as a construction guide. The model altar in Joshua 22 was to serve future generations as a reminder that those dwelling east of the Jordan were not ritually impure and had the right to come to the central sanctuary to make sacrifices. The response of the eastern tribes reflects the varied purposes of altars in ancient Israel: they were not only mounds for making sacrifices, but also signs of God's presence and identifying marks of a community devoted to God. Therefore, altars could be places of asylum (1 Kgs. 2:28) and could provide testimony of a certain identity. The latter purpose of the altar is reflected in Joshua 22. Sacrifice would be reserved for the central sanctuary, but the altar was a testimony of inclusion in the community that worshiped at the central site. The eastern tribes express concern that future generations on their land might say they have no "portion" in Israel (vv. 25, 27); the term "portion" (Hebrew *ḥeleq*) is often synonymous with "inheritance" (*naḥalah*; Josh. 15:13; 19:9; Ezek. 45:7). This shows again that the root problem was whether or not ownership of the land east of the Jordan was a sign of membership in the covenant community.

Membership in the Covenant Community

Joshua 22 speaks to the church's struggle with questions of holiness and purity in its membership, questions that have always threatened to divide the church, just as they posed barriers to the unity of the Israelite tribes. What marks the borders of the community of faith? Who in fact is worthy of membership? To what degree should the church "fence the table" to ensure only the pure in heart have access? What measure of openness and inclusiveness is appropriate within the community of faith? The story of the altar of witness does not answer these questions; it does, however, offer at least two potential guidelines on these matters. First, it depicts a group of tribes that so desire to preserve their place in the community of faith that they deceptively maneuver their way into communion; in effect, they act like Rahab (Josh. 2) and the Gibeonites (Josh. 9). Joshua 22, along with these stories from chapters 2 and 9, reports inclusion for those who will seek it by such extreme measures. In other words, Joshua stands on the side of openness for those who seek membership in the covenant community. Second, this story, like the accounts of Rahab and the Gibeonites, shows that all those who are included adhere to the Israelite creed. Before any defense of their actions, the tribes from Transjordan offer a doxological affirmation of faith: "The LORD, God of gods!" (v. 22) This essential declaration, which sets the Lord apart for complete and exclusive devotion, was Israel's ultimate test of inclusion. The church is left to work out its own central tenet or tenets of faith that determine who sits at the Lord's Table and who presides over it.

PART THREE

When the Lord Had Given Rest

Joshua 23—24

Joshua 23—24 records Joshua's final instructions for Israel's life in the land. These two chapters have often been viewed as two separate endings, reflective of "growth rings" in the book. Certainly chapters 23 and 24 are quite different in style. Whereas Joshua's address to Israel in chapter 24 is part of a ceremony in which Joshua acts as a prophetic mediator, his speech in chapter 23 is like the farewell addresses of other key leaders in the Deuteronomistic History. Moreover, Joshua 23 has significant parallels to chapter 1, creating a frame of references to torah faithfulness and making chapter 24 seem like a separate conclusion or epilogue. Nevertheless, the conclusion that Joshua 23 and 24 have nothing to do with each other would overlook unifying features. Both chapters include parting words that set Israel in the right mind for continuing after Joshua's death; moreover, Joshua 24:1 seems to assume that the gathering at Shechem follows immediately upon Joshua's speech in 23:2b–16. Therefore, it is appropriate to see these chapters as complementary, creating a single ending to the book.

Joshua 23
The Last Words of Joshua

In chapter 23 Joshua stands alongside Moses (Deuteronomy), Samuel (1 Sam. 12), and David (2 Sam. 23:1–7; 1 Kgs. 2:1–9) in offering a theological swan song that presses his people to maintain the torah faithfulness he has embodied. In order to evaluate the speech and its meaning for contemporary readers, this commentary will sketch out this chapter's place in its larger literary context, outline the speech's content and structure, and then inquire as to how the theological interests of this text might speak to people of faith today.

Literary Context and Function

Joshua 23 complements and parallels chapter 22, verses 2–5; chapter 23 is a farewell to all Israel, whereas the previous verses address only Reuben, Gad, and the half-tribe of Manasseh. The speech in chapter 23 is parallel to 22:2–5 in its pattern of first reminding Israel of God's gracious acts, then ordering them to observe the Mosaic torah. Moreover, Joshua 23, like 22:2–5, also reaches back to chapter 1 with theological interests that help frame the book as a whole. Several phrases and theological tenets found in chapter 1 reverberate through chapter 23: Joshua charges Israel, as God enjoined Joshua, to observe the precepts of a *written* document, the "book of the law of Moses" (1:8; 23:6); Israel is to maintain faithfulness to it, "turning aside from it neither to the right nor to the left" (1:7; 23:6); torah obedience is inextricably bound to success in obtaining and maintaining the land (1:7–8; 23:12–13, 16).

Although Joshua's speech in chapter 23 repeats and reaffirms many of the points made in chapter 1, this concluding address also prepares the reader for what will be encountered in the rest of the Deuteronomistic History. It carries warnings that failure to maintain strict obedience will result in God's refusal to drive out the nations before Israel and Israel will "perish quickly from the good land" (23:16). These admonitions temper the promises of possessing the land with the awareness of the "nations" that remain there (23:4, 7, 9, 12, 13). The previous section of the book (chaps. 13–22) contains statements of unqualified success (21:43–45), but chapter 23 seems intent on qualifying that euphoria in view of the story beyond Joshua. Concern over the nations' being a thorn in Israel's side and a snare for it looks forward specifically to Judges 2—16. The warning that Israel may perish from the good land because of these nations anticipates the defeat and exile of northern and southern kingdoms (2 Kgs. 17:7–23; 21:10–15). Hence Joshua 23 is a "major interpretive event" within the Deuteronomistic History with its broad view of the historical implications of torah obedience (Nelson, *Joshua*, p. 260). For that reason it may be read with other speeches that function similarly (Deut. 1—3; Josh. 1; 1 Sam. 12; 2 Sam. 7; 1 Kgs. 8).

Contents and Structure

Joshua's speech is set "a long time afterward" (v. 1). The lack of a specific date when Joshua spoke the words allows the reader to grasp what is really important to know about the setting, namely, that the speech came when the promised "rest" had been given to Israel (1:13, 15; 21:44; 22:4) and when Joshua had reached a ripe age. Joshua's advanced years gives an urgency to his words, as it did to his allotment of the land, set in the same geriatric circumstance (13:1).

The speech does not have an easily discernible outline but does divide naturally into two parts (vv. 2b–13, 14–16), both of which begin with Joshua's recognition of his old age (vv. 2b, 14a) and develop with similar rhetorical strategies. The first portion of the speech has a repeated sequence of motivational summaries (vv. 3–5, 9–10) followed by injunctions based on those summaries (vv. 6–8, 11–13). Verses 3–5 and 9–10 are like the book of Joshua in miniature. They report the capture and apportionment of the land, with emphasis on the fact that the Lord's action secured and continues to secure Canaan for Israel. This central claim is driven home by a line that appears (in Hebrew) exactly the same in both summaries: "it is the LORD your God who has fought/fights for you" (vv. 3, 10). The verb meaning "fought" is the same in Hebrew, but the translators assign different English tenses to fit their contexts. With this line these two sets of verses effectively state what may be the central theological claim of the book and prepare for the subsequent instructions.

Following both summaries are verses that exhort Israel to be faithful to Moses' commandments (vv. 6–8, 11–13), a type of charge typical of the book of Joshua. The specific legal requirement selected may surprise the reader, however, because it has not been mentioned specifically in the book heretofore. The concern expressed pertains to mixing with the nations that remain in the land (v. 7) and specifically with marrying their women (v. 12). Intermarriage itself is not the issue; rather, the point is that foreign wives will inevitably introduce foreign deities who will compete with the Lord for Israel's devotion (vv. 7, 13). This is a central concern of the Deuteronomist (Deut. 7:3–4), and the reason Solomon is judged harshly in 1 Kings 11:1–13.

Verse 7 contains four separate but related prohibitions regarding the gods of the nations left in the land. The first two instructions, concerning the names of the deities, may seem irrelevant to modern readers if the implications of the language are not clear. Therefore, some explanation may help us to appreciate the injunctions.

Joshua commands the Israelites not to "cause to remember" (NRSV "make mention") the names of the gods of the nations and then not to use them in oaths. The first instruction, whose exact implication is not clear, may simply refer to saying the name of a deity, as most translations indicate. At least two texts, however, raise the possibility that the concern is over setting up a memorial object with a god's name inscribed on it. Exodus 20:24 refers to the authentic place of worship as a site where the Lord causes his name to be remembered. A similar meaning for the same verb is found in 2 Samuel 18:18, in which Absalom sets up a pillar to recall his name, since he has no son to carry the name after him.

Regardless of the exact meaning of the remembrance of the deities' names, it is hard for modern readers to understand why the names themselves are such a focal point. The name represented the presence and power of the deity; hence, to swear an oath or offer a curse in the name of a god was to acknowledge the power of that god and attempt to tap into it. We see this in the command to abstain from making "wrongful use of the name of the LORD your God" (Exod. 20:7). Israel was to assume the name of its God was powerful but was ordered not to use the name for personal gain. They were not to use the names of other deities, because to do so would be to acknowledge their reality and efficacy (Deut. 6:13; 10:20).

The second section of Joshua's speech, like the first, summarizes the help God gave Israel to procure the land (v. 14) and then charges Israel with torah faithfulness (vv. 15–16). The tone of the exhortation, however, becomes decidedly negative and threatening in verses 14–16. The hortatory sections of the first portion of the speech are dominated by imperatives that call Israel to obedience ("be very steadfast," "be very careful"), but in verses 15–16 this style gives way to a set of conditional sentences and comparative statements that sound punitive: "just as all the good things," "the LORD will bring upon you all the bad things" (v. 15); "[i]f you transgress the covenant," "you shall perish quickly" (v. 16). Such threats appear or are implied in verses 6–8 and 11–13, but they become explicit in verses 15–16. They move like a wave from the placid sea of God's establishment of "rest" earlier in the book of Joshua (21:43–45) toward the uncertain future of Judges through Kings.

Retribution Theology

116

Joshua 23 is a parade example of what is sometimes called "retribution theology," a theology that presumes human action evokes an appropriate divine reaction, either reward or punishment. Consequently, many Christian readers disregard Joshua's speech, concluding that it expresses an archaic view of God's justice. They reason that tragedy befalls people of faith for the same reason it touches people with no faith, namely, because a broken creation yields unexplained circumstances that are sometimes negative. Scripture itself corrects any one-sided notion of evil always coming from God because of human disobedience (Job 42:7). Nevertheless, to pass over the theology of Joshua 23 too quickly would be to miss the other pole of biblical thought on this matter. Evil does sometimes arise because individuals or nations make wrong choices, choices that corrupt and remove them from divine intentions. Moreover, it would be theologically unhealthy to repudiate totally the notion of retributive justice; if God is not a judge who punishes sinfulness, can God really offer grace? Within such theological considerations Joshua 23 is a meaningful text for people of faith today. Punishment in this chapter does not preclude repentance and restoration. On the contrary, in the larger Deuteronomistic context the future for God's people in the land is always open, even though they may lose that land for a time (1 Kgs. 8:46–53).

Torah Obedience

Joshua 23 holds up the torah of Moses as the standard that determines whether or not Israel completely captures the land and remains in it. This chapter focuses on the negative implications of breaking torah; such unfaithfulness will cause Israel to "perish quickly from the good land" (v. 16). The speech implies, however, that the obverse is true as well. Success comes from observing and doing "all that is written in the book of the law of Moses, turning aside from it neither to the right nor to the left" (v. 6; see 1:7–8). If contemporary readers accept the notion of retributive justice, as discussed above, then Joshua 23 seems to present Scripture as the key to receiving God's blessings. To be sure, this notion can be misapplied to claim that God is bound to bless the one who observes biblical imperatives, but this application misses the point of Joshua's speech. Chapter 23 does not order Israel to obey the Mosaic legislation *in order that* God will bless them. True, the two ideas are linked, and ongoing success requires such faithfulness. Obedience to torah is ordered, however, because God has *already* given them the land and driven out their enemies. The key to the role of Scripture and obedience in the life of the believer is in the order of presentation in Joshua's address; in three cases (vv. 3–5, 9–10, 14) God's action on Israel's behalf is presented as *the reason* Israel should obey (vv. 6–8, 11–13, 15–16). This relationship between divine grace and

117

human response is particularly evident in the English translation of verses 6 and 11. NRSV renders a Hebrew conjunction (*waw*) with the English "therefore" to show that torah faithfulness comes as a response to God's gift already bestowed. Reversing the order of divine action/human response could open the door to a works righteousness that neither the New Testament nor the Old Testament supports.

The Issue of Marriage

The primary tenet of Deuteronomic law mentioned in Joshua 23 has often been misunderstood and misapplied. White separatists and other racist groups have used the command to keep separate from the nations in campaigns against interracial marriage, desegregation, and equal access to public buildings. In reality, the command in Joshua 23 has little or nothing to do with such issues; the problem in the book of Joshua is not ethnic purity but spiritual purity. Moreover, if the Deuteronomic concern over intermarriage expressed in verse 12 were taken as a literal injunction for today's society, it could probably be properly applied only by minority groups who struggle to maintain a distinct set of values rather than be assimilated into the dominant culture. Nevertheless, the focus on marriage as such misses the point; the instructions to keep separate from the nations are meant to reduce Israel's temptations to compromise and diminish its faith by mixing it with faith in other deities. The real issue is how people of faith will profess that faith in an environment that calls it into question. In the current eclectic religious environment, with a common denial of any absolute authority, the preacher should find ample opportunity to appropriate this portion of Joshua's speech.

Joshua 24
Choose Whom You Will Serve

"[C]hoose this day whom you will serve" (Josh. 24:15). This charge is the central theme of Joshua 24:1–28 and the last major theological injunction in the book. Joshua's stirring call to faithfulness, and the larger scene in which he makes it, is a grand culmination of many subjects presented previously. For example, the status of Joshua as Moses' successor reaches a peak here. As Joshua speaks, he is portrayed as a prophet like Moses, as arbiter of the covenant between God and Israel.

118

Most significant theologically, however, is the content of Joshua's call to God's people; his charge to choose the Lord is not only a fitting end to the book but presents what is arguably the central idea about God in the Old Testament. Indeed, the notion of exclusively serving the Lord refutes the polytheistic beliefs of Israel's neighbors, who thought there were multiple deities, each of whom represented some power. Joshua declares, in effect, that the Lord alone has power to save Israel and that therefore the Lord requires Israel's complete devotion.

Joshua 24 presents a host of challenges for interpreters. There are questions about how 24:1–28 is related to 8:30–35, about whether or not the account of Joshua's ceremony is a record of a historical event, and about how this section of the book is affiliated with the rest of the book and the literary strands in Genesis through Numbers. Such questions can obscure the theological significance of the text if they become the focus of interpretation. On the other hand, these questions can aid theological understanding of Joshua 24 and illuminate the message of this section of the book for people of faith. Thus we will focus on the issue of choosing the Lord, permitting the discussion of critical problems to inform us, in order to hear the call to Israel from Joshua to affirm its faith in the God of Abraham.

Why Shechem?

That geography sometimes serves theological purposes in the book of Joshua is nowhere more evident than in chapter 24. Shechem was associated closely with covenant making, a fact that helps explain why Joshua gathered the Israelites there for the ceremony reported in 24:1–28 (see 8:30–35). More importantly, Israel's patriarchs had a special connection to this city. Since God addressed Abraham for the first time in Canaan at Shechem (Gen. 12:7), this is a fitting place for Israel to gather when the promises to Abraham were fulfilled. Furthermore, Jacob's purchase of property near Shechem made it a proper burial site for Joseph's bones (Gen. 33:18–20), an act recorded in Joshua 24:32 immediately after the covenant-renewal ceremony. The most important ancestral link to Shechem for Joshua 24:1–28 is the story of Jacob there leading his household in an idol-burying ceremony (Gen. 35:2–4); Joshua's command to "put away the foreign gods that are among you" repeats verbatim a line Jacob spoke to his family (24:23; Gen. 35:2). This connection is important, since Joshua 24 is shaped around the idea of choosing the Lord and rejecting all other deities. Thus the geographical location of the command links Israel's attempts at faithfulness in Joshua's time to similar attempts of its ancestors.

119

Joshua's Prophetic Leadership

Joshua speaks as a prophet in 24:2–13. His "thus says the Lord" introductory formula tags the subsequent message as divine speech and identifies him as the Lord's messenger. Here Joshua stands clearly in the place Moses occupied in the previous generation, as mediator of the covenant between God and Israel (Exod. 19:3–6). So in one sense the portrait of Joshua in this final chapter is the loftiest of any in the book. After being carefully subordinated to Moses throughout much of the book, in 24:1 Joshua, like Moses on Mount Horeb, is the official arbiter of God's covenant with Israel. In this final chapter it appears that he has taken his place as the prophet "like Moses" spoken of in Deuteronomy 18:15 (but see the discussion of Josh. 1, "After the Death of Moses"). Nevertheless, it is important to remember what such an elevated position meant for Moses. Moses accepted the role of covenant mediator because the people realized that to see the fire of God on the mountain meant death. The great lawgiver agreed to stand between the people and God knowing that, as one "from among [the] people" (Deut. 18:15), he too would die after seeing God's glory (Olson, *Deuteronomy and the Death of Moses*, pp. 84–85). The portrait of Moses as mediator suggests two truths about prophetic leadership that apply to Joshua, as well as to any who aspire to the office of prophet: First, there is no room for the worship of the one who mediates between God and the human community. That person stands between God and the people as a human representative before God, not as a divine representative to humans. Mortals who bear the brunt of God's fire on behalf of the people are like all humans; they return to dust. Second, prophetic leadership has to do more with service than power, and the mediation role precipitates death (Deut. 1:9–18). To be sure, Joshua 24:1–28 does not mention Joshua seeing God's fire; nor does it say that Joshua's leadership causes his death. Still, Joshua is called "servant of the Lord" like Moses only at his death (Josh. 24:29), and his death is reported immediately after the covenant is sealed by his leadership (Josh. 24:29–30).

The Treaty Form in Joshua 24

The meaning of Joshua 24 is carried partly in its literary form. Many scholars have observed that verses 1–28 resemble certain ancient Near Eastern treaties, particularly the pacts the powerful Hittite empire made with its weaker neighbors. In these political contracts, dominant Hittite monarchs graciously entered into agreements of mutual faithfulness with vassals; the Hittites promised protection to the vassals, while demanding loyalty in return. Joshua 24:1–28 is similar in content and contains components virtually identical to these treaties: (1) When Joshua introduces the Lord as speaker in verse 2a, it resembles the preamble of Hittite treaties, in which the Hittite king is presented as the initiator of the agreement. (2) The Lord's reminder to Israel of how he established and maintained them to the present time (vv. 2b–13) is much like the treaties' historical prologue, in which the monarch recounts his gracious support of and protection for the vassal. (3) Joshua's call for Israel's faithfulness to God (vv. 14–15) and his establishment of stipulations (v. 25) is parallel to the section of Hittite treaties in which the king places expectations on the vassal. (4) The mention of witnesses in verses 22 and 27 parallels the Hittite king calling the gods to view the treaty. (5) Joshua's warning about the consequences of Israel breaking faith is broadly similar to the curses laid out in Hittite treaties. (6) Finally, the record of Joshua writing and displaying the covenant (vv. 26–27) is reminiscent of the Hittite provisions for storing and promulgating their political agreements (for an example of such a document see Pritchard, *Ancient Near Eastern Texts*, pp. 203–6).

This pattern of speech has profound implications. If indeed this section of Joshua has been patterned after secular diplomatic texts, it suggests that we should read 24:1–28 as a compact between God, the great ruler, and Israel, the helpless vassal. In other words, the form of the passage grounds the Israelite covenant in the metaphor of kingship. The treaty form invites the reader to think of God in poetic images such as shepherd, refuge, and judge; it encourages us to consider how Israel rejected theocracy when it took a human king (1 Sam. 8); it points forward to the teachings of Jesus that delineate human life and society in terms of God's rule.

Despite the similarities to ancient treaties, however, 24:1–28 does not contain a full record of such an agreement. This section of the book is a narrative. Verse 1 introduces the covenant ceremony and gives its setting; verse 28 concludes. Furthermore, the agreement itself is presented only in part. This indicates that the purpose of the passage is not to present a treaty, though the covenant-making event may be described in the familiar form of such an agreement. The text does not list specifically the statutes and ordinances Joshua made with Israel but only states that they were made (v. 25). Surely, if the author's goal was to report a treaty, the stipulations of the agreement would be spelled out. Additionally, the general comparison to Hittite treaties breaks down at two points: (1) The text says nothing of God's covenant obligations; instead it reports his graciousness in the past (vv. 2–13) as motivation for Israel's loyalty (vv. 14–15), and it emphasizes the Lord's

121

jealousy that will extinguish Israel if it is unfaithful. (2) It is not clear that the Lord is part of the covenant-making process. Rather, the ceremony reported in 24:1–28 seems to include a self-imposed obligation to the Lord. In other words, the text does not present a *demand* from God concerning Israel's obedience, as would be the case if 24:1–28 were reporting a treaty, but reflects Israel's own commitment to the Lord and the demands of their relationship with him. It seems rather the case that Joshua 24:1–28 utilizes the treaty form to emphasize the point that Israel must serve no gods other than the Lord. Each part of the narrative is geared toward that end: the memory of the Lord's past deeds sets Israel's God over against the gods of the nations (vv. 2–13); Joshua presents Israel's choice of the Lord as the overarching stipulation by which the people must live (vv. 14–15); the Israelites affirm that they will not serve any other gods (vv. 16–18); Joshua seals the covenant with a repetition of an earlier admonition to "put away the foreign gods" (v. 23). Hence, a basic outline of a treaty is used to drive home the key element of the Lord's demands on Israel.

The Contents of the Ceremony

The Lord's Benevolent Acts (vv. 2–13)

The first portion of the covenant ceremony is a recollection of the Lord's gracious acts towards Israel, told in order to evoke Israel's response of obedience and complete devotion. This section resembles Deuteronomy 26:5–9; Psalms 78; 105—106; and 136; and much study of Joshua 24:2–13 has centered on its comparison to these texts. Each of these passages begins with the story of Israel's ancestors, how they migrated from Mesopotamia and eventually became slaves in Egypt; then, the texts recall how God delivered the Israelites from bondage and established them in the land of Canaan. In light of these similarities, it has become common to think of Joshua 24:2–13 as a kind of creed. That is, this text was one of several formulae that served as an official statement of what Israel believed about God's beneficent care in the past (von Rad, *Old Testament Theology*, vol. 1, pp. 121–28).

Despite the usefulness of this generic view of verses 2–13, we must also pay attention to its distinctiveness and the fact that it is shaped to fit its context in Joshua. This section is unique among the historical summaries in the Old Testament in the way it focuses on the choice between the Lord and other gods. We see this particularly in comparison to the historical summary in Deuteronomy 26:5–9, which states rather matter-of-factly that the ancestors moved through Canaan, eventually lived in Egypt, and grew great in number: "A wandering Aramean was my ancestor; he went down to Egypt and lived there as an alien, few in number; and there he became a great nation, mighty and populous." Notice how this text emphasizes the ancestor's action: "he went down," "he lived there," "he became a great nation." But Joshua 24:3 is much more inclined to name God as the initiator and agent of success: "Then *I took your father* Abraham from beyond the River and *led him* through all the land of Canaan and *made his offspring many*." Indeed, to read verses 2–13 is to be overwhelmed by statements of God's action on Israel's behalf: "I took," "I gave," "I sent," "I brought out," "I handed over," "I rescued," "I gave." This emphasis on the Lord's initiative in forming Israel provides the foundation for the larger argument that it would be foolish to worship other gods, since this God is completely responsible for Israel's existence. Verses 2–13 provide a powerful prelude to the charge that follows, "[C]hoose this day whom you will serve" (v. 15).

The verbs that describe God's action in verses 2–13 stand out in relief against the terms that express human action. The words that communicate human activity depict either Israel's misdirected action that makes the Lord's action necessary (serving other gods, v. 2; going down to Egypt, v. 4), Israel's enemies' actions to which God responds (vv. 6, 8, 9, 11), or simply an innocuous action that moves the story along, like "lived beyond the Euphrates" (v. 2) or "lived in the wilderness" (v. 7). Certainly all purposeful action that brings blessing and salvation is exclusively that of the Lord. This message is driven home finally in verse 13 by way of a comparison of God's agency to Israel's inability to act for itself: "I gave you a land on which *you had not labored*, and towns *that you had not built*, and you live in them; you eat the fruit of vineyards and oliveyards *that you did not plant*." Hence, Joshua 24:2–13 portrays Israel on a divinely ordained and guarded journey on which Israel's success is attributed directly and completely to God.

Verses 2–3 are particularly important in the summary of God's mighty deeds, because they speak uniquely of the ancestral history in Mesopotamia and the fact that the patriarchs once worshiped other deities. Given this idolatrous background, ancient interpreters wondered why God took Abraham "from beyond the River." Could it be that Abraham rejected the idols of his father Terah and his brother Nahor? Was God motivated to choose Abraham because of his monotheistic tendencies? Some ancient readers thought so. The pseudepigraphical work known as the *Apocalypse of Abraham* reports that Abraham poked fun at the worship of idols. According to this book, Abraham thought idol worship was a ridiculous devotion to inanimate objects, and this conviction propelled Abraham into a campaign to destroy his father's gods (see the *Apocalypse of Abraham* chaps. 1, 3). These stories are

123

fascinating, but they read into Joshua 24:2–3 information that is not clearly intended, and furthermore such stories may miss the point altogether. The text of Joshua 24 seems to suggest that Abraham's break with "other gods" is initiated by God, not by Abraham's insightful rejection of idols. This is particularly evident when we compare Joshua 24:3 to the other Old Testament summaries of God's work for Israel. In the other texts that rehearse Israel's salvation history, the Lord is said to act first when he rescued Israel from slavery in Egypt. Joshua 24:3, on the other hand, traces God's work all the way back to the period in which the patriarchs lived in Mesopotamia: "I took your father Abraham from beyond the River." The implication is that Abraham would have continued to worship the gods of his father if God had not urged him towards a singular devotion. Hence Israel could not boast even of Abraham's piety; that also was due to God's graciousness.

The Charge to Faithfulness and Israel's Response (vv. 14–18)

Joshua's charge to Israel begins with two imperatives: "fear the LORD" (NRSV "revere") and "serve him" (v. 14). Sometimes the "fear of God" in the Old Testament refers to the reaction one would have when confronted by a theophany (Exod. 20:18; Deut. 5:5) or witnessing God's power demonstrated in historical acts (Isa. 25:3). Here, however, "fear" is used metaphorically. It does not suggest a literal quaking or cowering; instead, the term speaks of reverence that leads to devotion and obedience. Nevertheless, the literal notion of fear provides a backdrop for the figurative expression and is one essential aspect of any call to people of faith to commit to the Lord. To "fear the Lord" is to recognize the magnitude of God's demands, not to approach God casually as friend to friend, but reverently as subject to king. "Fear" in Joshua 24:14 denotes the posture of the heart necessary to pledge absolute faithfulness.

As important as the word "fear" is in Joshua's charge to Israel, the command to "serve" dominates this text. The term appears nine times in verses 14–18 and five more times in the rest of chapter 24. This word has two primary theological meanings, both of which are important for understanding this passage. First, in Joshua 24 "to serve" has the obvious sense of "to be devoted to." The verb is qualified by the expressions "in sincerity" and "in faithfulness." This description of complete devotion is much like the use of the verb in Deuteronomy 10:12 that calls for service "with all your heart and with all your soul"; the whole being is to give evidence of devotion to God. It may illuminate the verb to note that the nominal form of the same root means "slave" or "servant." The metaphor of the slave is helpful in that it speaks of exclusive "ownership" perhaps more clearly than any human relationship. A slave, who is at the complete disposal of the master and who has no independence or liberty apart from that given by the master, rightly models the absolute devotion being called for in verses 14–15 and which Israel promises in verses 16–18. In this sense Moses and Joshua are called "servant of the Lord" (Josh. 1:1; 24:29), and the apostle Paul refers to himself as a "slave of Jesus Christ" (Rom. 1:1; Phil. 1:1). Unlike human slavery, however, the servitude of which Joshua 24:14 speaks is not oppressive; instead, it leads to the full realization of life and blessing. Nevertheless, serving God is restrictive, and the limits imposed by such service are communicated in the structure of verse 14. Commands to serve the Lord appear near the beginning and at the end of the sentence, and between these two imperatives is the additional enjoinder to "put away the gods that your ancestors served beyond the River and in Egypt." Thus serving the Lord means *not* serving other gods; this is emphasized further in verse 15 when Joshua declares, "[C]hoose this day whom you will serve."

A second Old Testament use of the verb "to serve" is in reference to the performance of rituals in the sanctuary (Num. 8:11). This use of the word refers to outward acts that may be observed and measured, whereas the first use connotes an inward devotion. Most Christian readers devalue the notion that ritual performance is service, in part because some Old Testament prophets critique such "service" in Israelite worship at times as empty, devoid of sincere devotion (Isa. 43:23–24). To be sure, Joshua 24:14–18 uses the term "serve" with the first meaning, to refer to inner devotion to God. Inner devotion can be so vaporous, however, so vague and unmeasurable, that it is meaningless. Perhaps for that reason verse 14 recalls Genesis 35:2–4, in which Jacob leads a ceremony of collecting and burying idols (Gen. 35:4). Joshua 24:14 may suggest a ritual of removing the gods that might compete with the Lord as a sign of exclusive devotion. This can be important for contemporary people of faith who find it difficult to reject the pervasive societal and cultural influences that mitigate faith in God. Joshua 24:14 suggests that devotion can be more meaningful if it is made concrete in ritual; the act of burying idols not only enacts faith, it also gives public proclamation to one's commitment.

In verses 16–18 Israel responds to Joshua's charge to choose with a theological statement that borrows from the Lord's speech in verses 2–13. The response begins with Israel rejecting any notion of their serving other gods. Here the words "serve" and "abandon" are paired, in order to acknowledge that worshiping other deities constitutes apostasy (v. 16). Then Israel gives the motivation for maintaining devotion to God, namely, that the Lord has been Israel's savior in the past and continues

125

to perform mighty deeds on their behalf in the present (vv. 17–18a). This affirmation of faith mirrors verses 2–13 in that the speakers include themselves among the ones brought up from Egypt and kept safe in the wilderness (vv. 5–10). In reality they belong to a generation that did not experience the exodus, but their salvation is tied inextricably to that of their forebears. Verse 18 concludes Israel's response with a repetition of Joshua's declaration in verse 15, "[W]e also will serve the LORD," and a shared conviction, "he is *our* God." Here the Israelites state unambiguously that they stand with Joshua in his absolute devotion to the Lord and frame their choice of the Lord in response to Joshua's charge in verses 14–15.

"You Cannot Serve the LORD" (vv. 19–27)

To Israel's well-crafted and emphatic affirmation of their desire to serve the Lord, Joshua gives an arresting retort: "You cannot serve the LORD" (v. 19). The shift seems abrupt, and the tone so different from verses 14–18, that many scholars have proposed verses 19–24 were added by a later editor. Upon close examination, however, this section not only flows nicely with the previous verses but also completes the ideas expressed in verses 14–18. Indeed, verses 19–24 fill out the conception of God that is presented earlier in the chapter by explaining with great sharpness what it means to choose to serve the Lord and why it is so difficult. Joshua explains the impossibility of serving the Lord by saying first that "he is a holy God" (v. 19a). "Holy" is a word that sets God apart from the rest of the created order. In the context of Joshua's speech to Israel, it also connotes the Lord's demand for constant attention from humans who would serve him. Trent Butler astutely puts the demand of God's holiness in terms of the human being impressed by God's numinous and mysterious character (*Joshua*, p. 275). Because the worshiper is so impressed, he or she will attempt to imitate the purity of God but will recognize the inability to do so. This is at least part of what Joshua means when he says Israel cannot serve the Lord because of the Lord's holiness.

Joshua further defines the impossibility of serving God by saying, "He is a jealous God" (v. 19b). Herein lies what one Old Testament theologian rightly calls "the basic element in the whole Old Testament idea of God" (Eichrodt, *Theology of the Old Testament*, p. 210). Jealousy is so characteristic of Israel's God that it served as an official title, as Exodus 34:14 declares ("whose name is Jealous"). It is precisely God's jealousy that sets God apart from the gods Israel is to put away. In the polytheistic ancient Near East it was assumed that many deities would be worshiped and sacrificed to and their names invoked for whatever favor they were thought to give. These deities were not jealous, because their devotees also served other gods. Israel's God is unique; Israel's God expects absolute devotion. To comprehend the radical nature of this expectation and its singularity in ancient faith, the word "zealous" may be more accurate than the more common "jealous." The English word "zeal" communicates an aspect of God's nature that other terms may not capture; namely, God is not just jealous when Israel follows after other gods, but also zealous about the quality and depth of the relationship with Israel. The God of Israel demands the people to be fully engaged with him and to reflect his purity in every aspect of life. For this reason Joshua says Israel cannot meet God's demands. This expectation puts in perspective the statutes and ordinances Joshua made with Israel (v. 25); that is, Israel cannot fulfill its covenant obligation to God by simple adherence to a legal code. Rather, particular stipulations were illustrative examples of Israel's larger obligation to express God's holiness in every word and deed. The same declaration of the Lord's zeal appears in the explanation of the first commandment in Exodus 20:5 and Deuteronomy 5:9. This description of God dispels any notion that Old Testament faith is legalistic. Indeed, it frames the commandments as outward expressions of complete devotion to the Lord. In a similar way Jesus declared that the exclusive love of God is the summation of all the commandments (Matt. 22:36–40; Mark 12:28–34; Luke 10:25–28). Joshua makes clear that it is impossible to devote oneself completely to God, as God requires.

The zealousness of God, and the relational expectations that accompany it, perhaps can be comprehended only with analogy. A fitting similitude for modern people is the relationship of a person to a passionate lover. If the relationship leads to a marriage covenant, certain formal agreements apply. The obligation to the lover, however, is not fulfilled by mechanical compliance with stipulations. Imagine the absurdity of a partner in marriage greeting the spouse at the end of the day, "My commitment to you is complete today since I have not committed adultery." The relationship requires multiple expressions of love that can never be legislated fully. Moreover, the passion of the lover is naturally expressed as anger if the partner ignores or neglects the relationship.

This relational character of the covenant may explain why Joshua allows Israel to enter it despite his warning about God's jealousy. Following Joshua's words of caution is an almost antiphonal exchange between Joshua and the Israelites: The people declare again that they will serve the Lord (v. 21); Joshua makes them aware that their promise is, in effect, testimony against them if they turn to other gods, and the people acknowledge that fact (v. 22); then Joshua orders the Israelites again to "put away the foreign gods" (v. 23; see v. 14); finally, the people proclaim again, "The LORD our God we will serve," and then add a new promise, "him we will obey" (v. 24). Is there something in this interaction that makes it possible for Israel to serve the Lord or that softens God's demands? The people enact a rite in which they put away other gods, not the deities of the ancestors, but the foreign gods that are "among" the Israelites at the time of the ceremony. Hence they are not promising to eschew past apostasy, but present temptation to turn from God. The most significant key to Israel's action here, however, is the promise to obey the Lord; the phrase in Hebrew literally reads, "we will listen to his voice" (v. 24). This expression once again points to the relational aspect of the covenant. The Israelites cannot express complete devotion to God, but within the covenantal relationship they can be in constant conversation with God. In that conversation they experience grace as the Lord recognizes their inability to serve God. The rhetorical effect of verses 19–24 is that Israel in covenant stands under grace. This seems close to the notion expressed by Karl Barth that the human is under the Yes of God's justification, even though still under the No of divine judgment (*Church Dogmatics* IV, pp. 591–92). Joshua 24:19–24 seems to acknowledge that God gives God's Yes, even though God's No will always be present as well. Such is the nature of relationship with one who is zealous for intimacy, commitment, and faithfulness.

The Jealous God and Christian Faith

Joshua 24 speaks powerfully to the modern church. It may provide a model particularly for the branch of the church that conceives itself as a covenant community. When Joshua seeks to bind Israel to God in covenantal relationship, he insists that select ancestry is not sufficient; rather, children of the covenant must decide consciously and proclaim publicly that they will follow the God who claimed their mothers and fathers as devotees. The church today should approach baptism and confirmation with equal seriousness. But most importantly, this chapter urges upon the church a particular view of God. The primary characteristic of the Lord is zeal for those who would serve God, which makes God impossible to treat casually or to serve only when it seems convenient. Rather, this God requires complete devotion, and God's requirements carry threats for those who do not meet the demands.

Portions of Joshua 24:1–28 (vv. 1–3a, 14–15) are suggested for use at or near the end of the church's lectionary cycle. Thus the call to choose the Lord comes appropriately after the church celebrates Christ's birth, contemplates his sacrifice on the cross, and claims again his resurrection. The call of Joshua to Israel to "choose this day whom you will serve" is also the call to the contemporary community of faith. Christians should reflect on God's gracious acts on Israel's behalf as motivation for obedience (24:2–13). But the lectionary placement of the text in the church year suggests that our primary evidence for choosing the Lord is God's mighty acts in Christ; appropriately, John 6:56–69 is one of the New Testament texts paired with Joshua 24:1–3a, 14–15. John reports that many of Jesus' disciples ceased following him because they could not accept his radical message. But when Jesus asked the twelve if they too would abandon him, Peter replied, "Lord, to whom can we go? You have the words of eternal life" (John 6:68).

The summary of God's graciousness towards Israel in verses 2–13 speaks strongly to the church's doctrine of divine grace. As we have observed, the rehearsal of Israel's history in this text is shaped by the notion that Israel did nothing for itself; it owed its very existence to God. The land, which is here the primary sign of God's favor, was given to Israel solely because of God's act. "[I]t was not by your sword or by your bow," the Lord declares, that Canaan was taken (v. 12). But the text goes still further in its statement of God's exclusive prerogative, declaring that Israel depended upon the Lord even in the most rudimentary aspects of its origins that made possible the possession of the land. The summary supports what Augustine later calls prevenient grace; it purports that the very elemental decision to turn to the creator is the result of God's first endowing the human will with the desire and ability so to turn (*Saint Augustine: Letters*, vol. 5, no. 217).

Many readers never get the full impact of this text, however, since only one of the suggested lectionary readings includes verses 19–25. What makes this segment of Joshua so weighty theologically is that the emphasis on God's initiative in offering grace is complemented and tempered by statements of God's jealousy and stringent demands. Indeed, verses 19–24 show us that the fire of God that warms and comforts the chosen people can also burn them if they are unfaithful. The omission of verses 19–24 from the lectionary is unfortunate, because the warning about God's jealousy gives an important cast to the summary of God's salvific acts (vv. 2–13) and the call to serve the Lord (vv. 14–15). Although the threat of extermination (v. 20) for worshiping foreign gods may seem overly harsh, it reminds Israel that to enter covenant with God is to enter an intimate relationship. The benefits of the union cannot be enjoyed without the risk of the partner's wrath if the relational trust is breached. Some popular conceptions of God exclude God's demands and the inherent threats of being in relationship with God. When verses 19–24 are left out of the portrait of God's covenant, however, what remains is a diminished idea of relationship with the divine. The church needs to measure its proclamation of God's character against the picture we find in Joshua 24, particularly verses 19–20. Too often the church promotes an understanding of God that is influenced more by Enlightenment ideals than by Scripture. Indeed, the zealous God of this text is often put away in favor of a detached clock-maker god; this common perception of God allows the divine to be seen as love without judgment, as kindness without expectation. Such a God has no passion; Joshua's God does. Moreover, the text implies that this zealous God expects Israel to be passionate as well. In its discussion of the First Commandment the Westminster Catechism aptly lists among the expectations to fulfill the command "to be zealous" (*The Constitution of the Presbyterian Church [U.S.A.], Part I, Book of Confessions* 7.214). Indeed, the implication of God's zealousness is that the person of faith must also be zealous for God. At no time can the relationship with God be put on automatic pilot; in no way can the demands of the relationship be met by compliance to a code of ethics, even though such a code may be useful as illustration and reminder of God's expectations. The person in relationship with this God must, in every moment of life, choose whether to be faithful to God or to some competing reality. In sum, God's zealousness requires people of faith to "love the LORD your God with all your heart, and with all your soul, and with all your might" (Deut. 6:5). This message is at the heart of the book of Joshua, and at the heart of the gospel.

SELECTED BIBLIOGRAPHY

For Further Study

Auld, A. Graeme. *Joshua, Moses, and the Land: Tetrateuch-Pentateuch in a Generation since 1938*. Edinburgh: T. & T. Clark, 1980.

———. *Joshua Retold: Synoptic Perspectives*. Old Testament Studies. Edinburgh: T. & T. Clark, 1998.

Boling, Robert and G. Ernest Wright. *Joshua*. Anchor Bible 6. New York: Doubleday, 1982.

Bright, John. *A History of Israel*. 4th ed. Louisville, Ky.: Westminster John Knox Press, 2000.

Butler, Trent C. *Joshua*. Word Biblical Commentary, vol. 7. Waco, Tex.: Word Books, 1983.

Calvin, John. *Commentaries on the Book of Joshua*. Grand Rapids: Wm. B. Eerdmans, 1948.

Campbell, Antony F. and Mark A. O'Brien. *Unfolding the Deuteronomistic History: Origins, Upgrades, Present Text*. Minneapolis: Fortress Press, 2000.

Davis, Ellen F. "Critical Traditioning: Seeking an Inner Biblical Hermeneutic." *Anglican Theological Review* 82 (2000): 733–51.

Fretheim, Terence. *Deuteronomic History*. Nashville: Abingdon Press, 1983.

Gottwald, Norman. *The Tribes of Yahweh: A Sociology of the Religion of Liberated Israel, 1250–1050 B.C.E.* London: SCM Press, 1980.

Greenspoon, L. J. *Textual Studies in the Book of Joshua*. Harvard Semitic Monographs 28. Chico, Calif.: Scholars Press, 1983.

Hawk, L. Daniel. *Joshua*. Berit Olam: Studies in Hebrew Narrative and Poetry. Collegeville, Minn.: Liturgical Press, 2000.

Mayes, A. D. H. *The Story of Israel between Settlement and Exile*. London: SCM Press, 1983.

Mazar, Amihai. *Archaeology of the Land of the Bible, 10,000–586 B.C.E.* New York: Doubleday, 1990.

McBride, S. Dean, Jr. "Polity of the Covenant People." *Interpretation* 41 (1987): 229–44.

Nelson, Richard D. *The Historical Books*. Nashville: Abingdon Press, 1998.

———. *Joshua, A Commentary*. Old Testament Library. Louisville, Ky.: Westminster John Knox Press, 1997.

———. "Josiah in the Book of Joshua." *Journal of Biblical Literature* 100 (1981): 531–40.

Niditch, Susan. *War in the Hebrew Bible: A Study in the Ethics of Violence*. New York: Oxford University Press, 1993.

Noth, Martin. *The Deuteronomistic History*. Journal for the Study of the Old Testament Supplement Series 15. Sheffield: Sheffield Academic Press, 1981.

Polzin, Robert. *Moses and the Deuteronomist: A Literary Study of the Deuteronomistic History*. New York: Seabury Press, 1980.

Rad, Gerhard von. *The Problem of the Hexateuch and Other Essays*. Edinburgh: Oliver & Boyd, 1966.

Soggin, J. Alberto. *Joshua, A Commentary*. Old Testament Library. Philadelphia: Westminster Press, 1972.

Stone, Lawson G. "Ethical and Apologetic Tendencies in the Redaction of the Book of Joshua." *The Catholic Biblical Quarterly* 53 (1991): 25–36.

Van Seters, John. *In Search of History*. Louisville, Ky.: Westminster John Knox Press, 1982.

———. "Joshua's Campaign of Canaan and Near Eastern Historiography." *Scandinavian Journal of the Old Testament* 2 (1990): 1–12.

Wenham, G. J. "The Deuteronomic Theology of the Book of Joshua." *Journal of Biblical Literature* 90 (1971): 140–48.

Literature Cited

Albright, William Foxwell. *The Excavation of Tell Beit Mirsim*. Vol. 3, *The Iron Age*. New Haven, Conn.: American Schools of Oriental Research, 1943.

Auld, A. Graeme. *Joshua, Judges, and Ruth*. Daily Study Bible. Philadelphia: Westminster Press, 1984.

———. *Joshua, Moses, and the Land: Tetrateuch-Pentateuch in a Generation since 1938*. Edinburgh: T. & T. Clark, 1980.

Barth, Karl. *Church Dogmatics*. IV, *The Doctrine of Reconciliation*, Part 1. Edinburgh: T. & T. Clark, 1956.

Berkhof, Hendrikus. *Christian Faith: An Introduction to the Study of the Faith*. Translated by Sierd Woudstra. Grand Rapids: Wm. B. Eerdmans, 1979.

Bettenson, Henry, ed. *Documents of the Christian Church*. 2d ed. Oxford: Oxford University Press, 1963.

Brueggemann, Walter. *Revelation and Violence: A Study in Contextualization*. Milwaukee: Marquette University Press, 1986.

Butler, Trent C. *Joshua*. Word Biblical Commentary, vol. 7. Waco, Tex.: Word Books, 1983.

Callaway, Joseph A. "Ai." In *Anchor Bible Dictionary*. Edited by David Noel Freedman. 6 vols. New York: Doubleday, 1994.

Calvin, John. *Commentaries on the Book of Joshua*. Grand Rapids: Wm. B. Eerdmans, 1948.

Childs, Brevard S. "A Study of the Formula 'Until This Day.'" *Journal of Biblical Literature* 82 (1963): 279–92.

Cross, Frank Moore. *Canaanite Myth and Hebrew Epic: Essays in the History of the Religion of Israel*. Cambridge, Mass.: Harvard University Press, 1973.

Davis, Ellen F. "Critical Traditioning: Seeking an Inner Biblical Hermeneutic." *Anglican Theological Review* 82 (2000): 733–51.

Eichrodt, Walther. *Theology of the Old Testament*. Philadelphia: Westminster Press, 1961.

Fretheim, Terence. *Deuteronomic History*. Nashville: Abingdon Press, 1983.

Ginsberg, Louis. *The Legends of the Jews*. 6 vol. Philadelphia: Jewish Publication Society of America, 1913.

Gottwald, Norman. *The Hebrew Bible: A Socio-Literary Introduction*. Philadelphia: Fortress Press, 1985.

Gustafson, James M. *Treasure in Earthen Vessels: The Church as a Human Community*. New York: Harper & Bros., 1961.

Hawk, L. Daniel. *Joshua*. Berit Olam: Studies in Hebrew Narrative and Poetry. Collegeville, Minn.: Liturgical Press, 2000.

Henry, Matthew. *An Exposition of the Old and New Testaments*. Vol. 2. Edinburgh: C. MacFarqhar and Co., 1708.

Hoffman, Yair. "The Deuteronomistic Concept of the Herem." *Zeitschrift für die alttestamentlicheWissenschaft* 111 (1999): 196–210.

Holladay, John S., Jr. "The Day(s) the Moon Stood Still." *Journal of Biblical Literature* 87 (1968): 166–78.

Kierkegaard, Søren. *Philosophical Fragments*. 2d ed. Translated by D. F. Swenson. Princeton, N.J.: Princeton University Press, 1962.

Mays, James Luther. "Justice: Perspectives from the Prophetic Tradition." *Interpretation* 37 (1983): 5–17.

Mazar, Amihai. *Archaeology of the Land of the Bible, 10,000–586 B.C.E.* New York: Doubleday, 1990.

McBride, S. Dean, Jr. "Polity of the Covenant People." *Interpretation* 41 (1987): 229–44.

McCarthy, Dennis J. "An Installation Genre?" *Journal of Biblical Literature* 90 (1971): 31–41.

Miller, Patrick D. *The Divine Warrior in Early Israel*. Cambridge, Mass.: Harvard University Press, 1973.

———. *Deuteronomy*. Interpretation: A Bible Commentary for Teaching and Preaching. Louisville, Ky.: John Knox Press, 1990.

Nelson, Richard D. *The Historical Books*. Nashville: Abingdon Press, 1998.

———. *Joshua, A Commentary*. Old Testament Library. Louisville, Ky.: Westminster John Knox Press, 1997.

———. "Josiah in the Book of Joshua." *Journal of Biblical Literature* 100 (1981): 531–40.

Niditch, Susan. *War in the Hebrew Bible: A Study in the Ethics of Violence*. New York: Oxford University Press, 1993.

Noort, Ed. *Das Buch Josua: Forschungsgeschichte und Problemfelder*. Darmstadt: Wissenschaftliche Buchgesellschaft, 1998.

Olson, Dennis T. *Deuteronomy and the Death of Moses: A Theological Reading*. Overtures to Biblical Theology. Minneapolis: Fortress Press, 1994.

———. *Numbers*. Interpretation: A Bible Commentary for Teaching and Preaching. Louisville, Ky.: John Knox Press, 1996.

Origen. *Homélies sur Josué*. Sources Chrétiennes, no. 71. Paris: Tour-Maubourg, 1960.

Paine, Thomas. *The Age of Reason*. Secaucus, N.J.: Citadel Press, 1997.

Parsons, Wilfrid, S. N. D., trans. *The Fathers of the Church,* vol. 32: *Saint Augustine: Letters,* vol. 5 (204–270). New York: Fathers of the Church, Inc., 1956.

Perdue, Leo G., Joseph Blenkinsopp, John J. Collins, and Carol Meyers. *Families in Ancient Israel*. The Family, Religion, and Culture Series. Louisville, Ky.: Westminster John Knox Press, 1997.

Polzin, Robert. *Moses and the Deuteronomist: A Literary Study of the Deuteronomistic History*. New York: Seabury Press, 1980.

Pritchard, J. B., ed. *Ancient Near Eastern Texts Relating to the Old Testament*. 3d ed. Princeton, N.J.: Princeton University Press, 1969.

Rad, Gerhard von. *Old Testament Theology*. Vol. 1, *The Theology of Israel's Historical Traditions*. New York: Harper & Row, 1962.

Schroeder, Christoph O. *History, Justice, and the Agency of God: A Hermeneutical and Exegetical Investigation on Isaiah and Psalms*. Biblical Interpretation Series, vol. 52. Leiden: Brill, 2000.

Smend, Rudolf. "Das Gesetz und die Völker: Ein Beitrag zur deuteronomistischen Redactionsgeschichte." In *Probleme biblischer Theologie*. Edited by Hans Walter Wolff. Munich: Chr. Kaiser Verlag, 1971, pp. 494–509.

Soggin, J. Alberto. *Joshua, A Commentary*. Old Testament Library. Philadelphia: Westminster Press, 1972.

Spurgeon, Charles Haddon. *The Treasury of the Bible*. Vol. 1. Grand Rapids: Baker Book House, 1981.

Stone, Lawson G. "Ethical and Apologetic Tendencies in the Redaction of the Book of Joshua." *The Catholic Biblical Quarterly* 53 (1991): 25–36.

Terrien, Samuel. *The Elusive Presence: Toward a New Biblical Theology*. San Francisco: Harper & Row, 1978.

Van Seters, John. *In Search of History*. Louisville, Ky.: Westminster John Knox Press, 1982.

———. "Joshua's Campaign of Canaan and Near Eastern Historiography." *Scandinavian Journal of the Old Testament* 2 (1990): 1–12.

Verhey, Allen D. "The Holy Bible and Sanctified Sexuality: An Evangelical Approach to Scripture and Sexual Ethics." *Interpretation* 49 (1995, no. 1): 31–45.

Wesley, John. *John Wesley's Commentary on the Bible*. Edited by G. Roger Schoenhals. Grand Rapids: Francis Asbury Press, 1990.